My Answer to Cancer

AN INSPIRATIONAL STORY ABOUT LIFE

CATHY BROWN

BALBOA.
PRESS

A DIVISION OF HAY HOUSE

Balboa Press books may be ordered through booksellers or by contacting:

Balboa Press
A Division of Hay House
1663 Liberty Drive
Bloomington, IN 47403
www.balboapress.com.au
1 (877) 407-4847

Because of the dynamic nature of the Internet, any web addresses or
links contained in this book may have changed since publication and
may no longer be valid. The views expressed in this work are solely those
of the author and do not necessarily reflect the views of the publisher,
and the publisher hereby disclaims any responsibility for them.

The author of this book does not dispense medical advice or prescribe the use
of any technique as a form of treatment for physical, emotional, or medical
problems without the advice of a physician, either directly or indirectly. The
intent of the author is only to offer information of a general nature to help
you in your quest for emotional and spiritual well-being. In the event you use
any of the information in this book for yourself, which is your constitutional
right, the author and the publisher assume no responsibility for your actions.

Any people depicted in stock imagery provided by Thinkstock are models,
and such images are being used for illustrative purposes only.
Certain stock imagery © Thinkstock.

Print information available on the last page.

ISBN: 978-1-5043-0494-8 (sc)
ISBN: 978-1-5043-0495-5 (e)

Balboa Press rev. date: 11/04/2016

To my children, Carolyn and Hayden.
It was my deep love for both of you that fuelled my will to live.

FOREWORD

We live in an age of information overload. So many books. So many websites, apps, online courses. So many people and groups offering so much—some authentic; some clearly misinformed, some clearly with vested interests.

So for anyone newly diagnosed with cancer there is a critical question. Who can you trust? Who is genuine? Who can you turn to for reliable information? Who can you learn from with confidence?

In Tibet, there is a famous saying: "An old patient is more useful than a young doctor." Of course it is important to be clear that Tibetans hold doctors in high regard, but you probably get the point. Direct experience counts for a lot.

Cathy Brown is one of those authentic people who has been through a lot. First diagnosed with melanoma in 1989, Cathy was confronted with her cancer returning just one year later. She faced the prospect of an early and untimely death. Now a genuine, long-term cancer survivor, it is fair to say that during the years of her recovery, Cathy was required to meet most of the challenges cancer is capable of presenting.

Naturally there were highs and lows, and Cathy recounts them in a personal, open, humorous, heartfelt fashion. But more than being a mere retelling of events, Cathy's book treats us to one useful tip after another. This she combines with anecdotes from her many years of helping others, in a way that builds into a practical guide to good health and well-being.

For not only did Cathy find a way to survive against the odds, she went on to study and to further develop the knowledge of Mind-Body Medicine she had initially gained through her own direct experience.

An old patient may well be "more useful than a young doctor" as the saying goes, but Cathy is also a well-experienced clinician. Almost as soon as she had recovered, Cathy was powerfully motivated to share her experience and what she had learnt with others.

She found the opportunity to do so through working with Cancer Support WA, and over the last twenty years, Cathy has continued to learn from the thousands of people affected by cancer who she has helped.

What stands out? Cathy's story offers hope. Real hope. Hope that is backed by her own experience, her years of experience working with others, and all the study Cathy has done along the way. So this is genuine hope. There is so much a person diagnosed with cancer can do to make a difference in how they feel, how the disease progresses; in their own recovery; and, amid all the challenges the disease can create, in finding meaning in life.

Also, Cathy speaks from experience when she emphasises that, in every situation, there are choices, and when faced with making a decision, there are always more choices than you first thought. She recounts the processes she went through as she struggled to clarify and decide upon the many choices she faced during her own recovery. This provides practical insight into how we may sort out what to do when faced with our own difficult but crucial choices.

Having the privilege of knowing Cathy for many years, and having enjoyed working together with her on several occasions, I know Cathy is authentic. She is someone who can be trusted—someone who has a great depth of experience to draw upon, a wealth of knowledge, a good heart, and a genuine motivation to help others.

So there is a real sense of excitement in being able to introduce Cathy's book, *My Answer to Cancer: An Inspirational Story about Life.*

Finally she has done it! For many years, many people, including myself, have urged Cathy to write of her experiences and knowledge. We knew what she had to offer. Yet Cathy bided her time. My sense is she understood the value of gathering long-term experience before speaking out. Now there is genuine long-term survival to speak of. Now there is genuine long-term experience gathered from working with many others to speak of.

This then is a book that everyone involved with cancer will benefit from reading.

In this age of technological overload, for anyone wondering where they can turn for genuine, trustworthy information on how to transform the many potential difficulties that cancer presents, I heartily recommend Cathy Brown and her book, *My Answer to Cancer: An Inspirational Story about Life*.

Be inspired. Be informed. Read it!

Ian Gawler OAM
Yarra Junction
June 2016

CHAPTER 1

The Diagnosis

I t is hard to imagine that a tiny red dot on my right forearm would change my life so dramatically. It was June 1989, and I was a healthy thirty-two-year-old woman, happily married to Bob and the mother of two young children—Carolyn (seven) and Hayden (five). I was in my kitchen busily putting the dishes away when I knocked this tiny red dot, and a shot of pain travelled up my arm.

The next time I visited the doctor, I told him about this experience. He examined the unusual skin blemish and said, "No, that's all right. Don't worry about it."

I didn't feel comfortable with his response so asked him kindly to go ahead and remove it.

He replied, "Oh, all right, if it will keep you happy."

So off we went to another part of the surgery, and he excised it. I had four stitches and went home.

The next morning, I received a phone call from the doctor asking me how I was. My first thought was, *Wow, I haven't had service like this before*, and then the penny dropped. This wasn't a courtesy call to enquire about my well-being; he was calling to tell me that the insignificant-looking red dot on my arm was a melanoma.

My stomach turned and tightened like I had received a severe blow. My greatest fear was melanoma! *Is this really happening to me?*

1

When I was thirteen, a family friend had died three months after giving birth to her baby girl. Kay had had a melanoma removed a couple of years previously and thought nothing more about it. When she became pregnant, the melanoma took over and spread rapidly throughout her body. Everyone was devastated when she died, leaving a loving husband and her delightful baby. Life appeared to me to be very unfair and, witnessing this event at such a young age created a fear of melanoma deep within me. Now, I was facing this same diagnosis.

The doctor requested that I return to the surgery, where he was arranging for me to have a wider excision to ensure all of the melanoma was removed. After the plastic surgeon made the wider excision to ensure clearance, he skilfully pulled my skin back together, although it looked as though a vicious creature had taken a bite out of my arm. Over the years, I'd had many dark moles and freckles removed, but the biopsies had always showed they were benign, so it hadn't occurred to me that a melanoma could be raised red and look like a pimple. Five years earlier, I had woken up after an unrelated operation with numerous wounds and stitches all over my body. It looked like someone had gone mad and stabbed me. I had asked the doctor to remove any suspicious moles while I was under the anaesthetic, and he had certainly done that. I'd joked at the time that, if I'd had a drink of water, I would have looked like a leaking sieve.

Now with this diagnosis, I was terrified. Desperate for knowledge, I visited the Western Australian Cancer Foundation and asked what I could do to help myself and hopefully not have the melanoma spread. The woman I spoke with just looked at me in surprise and said, "There's nothing you can do. You just have to wait and see."

Great! It felt like I was stuck on a railway track, and all I could see was a train coming straight for me. I couldn't get off, and there was no one to assist me. There was a pleading from within. *Help! Someone, please help me.*

Initially, my life continued normally as a busy mum, but over the next couple of months, my right underarm became tight. I returned to the doctor, and after examining me, he said that he couldn't feel anything. He put the tight sensation I was experiencing down to damaged nerves from the surgery. Nevertheless, the discomfort continued. I returned again for an examination, but still nothing. The doctor, through his body language and comments, made me feel as though I was being paranoid.

In March 1990, my legs broke out in large, inflamed, bright-red blisters. My legs looked like they had been badly burnt. Back to the doctor, and yet again there were no answers. *Where are the answers?* He called in two of his colleagues to have a look. There I was with three doctors examining my legs and all agreeing that they hadn't seen anything like it—the blisters, not the legs! The rest of my body appeared just fine, but it was really strange that my legs were covered in these watery blisters. I asked the doctors if this could be related to the melanoma.

"No," they assured me.

I knew deep down within me something was seriously wrong. Blisters like these don't just appear on a normal, healthy body.

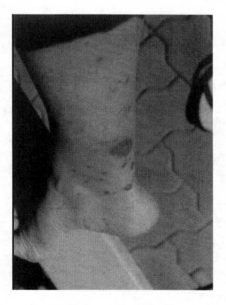

Bullous pemphigoid

I was referred to a dermatologist, who was equally perplexed by the blisters. He excised one and sent it to the laboratory.

Again I inquired, "Is this related to the melanoma?"

"No," he assured me.

The dermatologist phoned me a couple of days later with the results. "It's a disease called bullous pemphigoid."

I asked him what that was and he answered, "We don't really know. It is very rare and usually happens to old people just before they die."

What! I'm only thirty-three, and I don't intend to die now.

After many visits, potions, and lotions, the blisters finally cleared up, but I noticed that the tightness and discomfort under my arm were becoming extreme. *Perhaps I can also feel some swelling, or am I just being paranoid?* In any case, I was worried—very worried!

Within a week or so, I knew it was not my imagination. When I lifted my arm, a lump the size of a golf ball would appear. When I put my arm down, it disappeared. Panic was really starting to set in now.

As I was having a small skin cancer removed by the same plastic surgeon as before, I asked him about the lump. He suggested I return to my GP, who examined me and recommended that I see a surgeon at the hospital ASAP.

After examining me, the surgeon stated that I did have a large mass under my right arm and that it must be removed immediately. He spoke to another surgeon, who had informed him that the operating list for the following Thursday was full, and his answer to this was, "Get rid of someone."

It gives you a horrible feeling when you look down at your medical file and see a big red "Urgent" sticker slapped across the front. My heart pumped faster, and my stomach churned. This was when I knew for certain that my life was about to be turned upside down.

I mentioned the bullous pemphigoid to him and asked his opinion. He told me that, in his opinion, my immune system was so locked into fighting the tumours that it had broken down, and the blisters were the manifestation of that struggle. I wondered why my body had responded in this particular way. At least I had an answer now. Somehow, the answer provided little comfort.

I was in hospital for five days after the operation that took place on May 3, 1990. Staying optimistic during these days was challenging, and always in the back of my mind, I was waiting for someone to walk in and say, "Sorry, Cathy, this has all been a big mistake, and there is nothing wrong with you." Unfortunately, that person never turned up.

I also found filling in the long hours while waiting until I could be discharged very difficult. Everything felt so sterile, and the air smelt stale from the disinfectants. One afternoon, I decided to go for a walk, dragging the metal trolley supporting the draining bag from my wound. I caught the lift to the second floor, where there was an outdoor area for people to sit in the fresh air. The area was bare except for a couple of large pots containing struggling plants. As I sat there in solitude, contemplating my future, a butterfly appeared from nowhere and fluttered around while looking for somewhere to land. It reminded me of a movie I had seen when I was a child. The story relayed that, if a butterfly landed on you, everything would turn out okay.

Then I could not believe it. As I was sitting on the chair reminiscing about this movie, the butterfly flew over and landed on my shoulder. I quietly turned my head to watch as it sat there and rested, slowly flapping its wings backward and forward. I fervently hoped that this was a good omen for me and that everything would turn out okay.

After I was discharged from hospital, my husband, Bob, and I returned the following Friday for the official results. We walked into the doctor's office. It was stark and bare, with a few files on the desk that the doctor sat behind, not daring to look me in the eyes. It felt like being sent before a judge, to see if the verdict was guilty or not guilty for some crime I did not commit. Here was someone who was going to tell me whether I would live or die—whether I would be released on a good behaviour bond or given the death sentence. *What have I done wrong in my life to deserve this? Why me?* The anger was beginning to surface. My children were only six and eight years old. They needed their mum, and I wanted to be there to see them grow up. There was a strong sense of injustice within me. After waiting anxiously for the doctor for over two hours, my mind had rehearsed a thousand scenarios, and my nerves were shot. Finally, the results were delivered.

The report stated that metastatic tumour was present extensively in two of the lymph nodes removed from my right axillary. The largest mass was five centimetres in diameter.

Most of the following conversation was a blur. Everything was in slow motion, and emotionally I went numb with this news. My mind could not take this information in and process it straight away. It is impossible to emotionally and mentally prepare for something like this. I believe everyone fears being given a diagnosis of cancer. The first time was really hard, but now the second time was devastating. *What questions should I ask him? How should I respond?* Thoughts, thoughts, thoughts, so many of them! I wanted them to go away. I was confused by the mental activity racing crazily around.

My first question was, "How long do I have to live?"

He replied, "I'm not sure, maybe a couple of months, perhaps a couple of years."

I am not one to swear much, but I remember thinking, *Bugger* (and a few other descriptive words)! I then asked what would finally finish me off.

His emotionless response will always haunt me. "It will go to your lungs, liver, or brain. You will be referred to an oncologist. He will monitor your progress. In your situation, chemotherapy is unlikely to help. Since you are young, with a young family, you would be better off going home and enjoying whatever time you have left while you are well."

My thoughts rushed back to my experience with the butterfly, and I realised that, obviously, my belief about the butterfly landing on my shoulder was wrong. Everything *wasn't* going to turn out okay.

I left feeling gutted; I don't really remember anything about the walk from the hospital to the car, but I do remember that we received a parking fine because I had been waiting for over two hours for the doctor to see me.

I asked Bob to drive me to the beach, as I needed time to gather myself together. I felt like I had been slammed into a brick wall and was totally shattered as I sat in the car and sobbed. Thoughts and emotions overwhelmed me. *I don't want to die. I want to live. I don't want to leave my family. I want to be with them. I don't want to die and leave my children. I want to see them grow up. Bob can always get another wife, but no one will ever love my children like I do.* They were only young and needed me. I couldn't leave them. They were my reason to live.

*   *   *

Mother's Day was two days later, and it was one of the hardest days of my life. Nothing could have prepared me for how difficult it would be to face my children, not knowing whether this was my last Mothers' Day with them. I woke up during the night shaking. The images flashing through my mind can possibly be imagined but only understood by someone who has been in this situation. No words or description can accurately express what I went through. It was horrendous. I didn't know where to turn or what to do.

Again I went to see my GP for help. His answer to my distress was to prescribe me a sedative (Serapax) for my nerves and tell me to send in the rest of the family to see him if they needed any help to cope. This was not the type of help I was looking for; I didn't want to be drugged out so I couldn't feel my emotional and mental pain or function and make rational decisions about my life. I needed guidance and emotional support, and I certainly wasn't going to get that through drugs.

My heart was racing, and it took a lot of courage to walk into the oncologist's office. My mum came with me on this occasion. The doctor looked at her and started a conversation, assuming that, as my mother was older, she was the one with cancer and that I had come to support her. I tactfully informed him that I was the one with cancer.

He stopped, reread my file, shook his head in a disapproving manner from side to side, clicked his tongue, and simply said, "You're in the hands of fate."

I was really shocked and angry at his cold response and remember thinking, *You don't know who you are dealing with, mate! Don't just treat me as another faceless statistic.*

But as fate would have it, I would later be thankful to him for being so blunt and triggering something inside of me that said, if fate has anything to do with this, I'm going to give it all the help it needs!

Within the darkness of this shock and confusion, I realised that I had to take responsibility for my own health and, ultimately, my life. From somewhere deep within me came the question, *Is there another way?*

I didn't know if there was, but I knew I was about to embark on a journey of self-discovery to find *my answer to cancer.* The trouble was, I didn't have a clue where to begin.

DEPARTMENT OF HISTOPATHOLOGY

LAB NO : ....
90H1485 to 90H1486

Ward/Clinic **B8S**	
Medical Officer	
Pathologist	

Surname **BROWN**	UMRN **H3162661**	Sex **F**
Forenames **CATHRYN**		Birthdate **01/08/1956**

Lymphadenopathy. Had recent melanoma removed from right forearm.

Date of Request : 03/05/1990

90H1485 : RIGHT AXILLARY MASS
90H1486 : RIGHT APICAL LYMPH NODE

MACROSCOPIC DESCRIPTION'S :

90H1485: Specimen is a group of lymph nodes with surrounding fatty tissue which measures 9 x 6 x 4 cms. There are at least six lymph nodes in the specimen and the largest node is about 5 cms in diameter. Two lymph nodes including the largest one are obviously largely replaced by whitish tumour mass.

90H1486: Specimen is a 12 x 5 x 5 mms oval firm lymph node which has already been divided into two with some attached fatty tissue.

MICROSCOPIC DESCRIPTION'S :

90H1485 : Sections show metastatic tumour present extensively in the larger lymph node and also throughout a medium size lymph node with extensive sinusoidal infiltration. The tumour exhibits bizarre cytologic features with multinucleated giant cells, spindle shaped cells and some cuboidal cells. There is abundant amphophilic cytoplasm with vesicular nuclei and prominent nucleoli including intranuclear inclusions. Atypical giant cells are easily identified, however, no definite pigment is seen.

90H1486 : Sections of the lymph node show mild reactive changes only. No evidence of metastatic tumour is seen.

CONCLUSION 90H1485 :

RIGHT AXILLA MASS : METASTATIC TUMOUR IS PRESENT EXTENSIVELY IN TWO OF SIX DRAINING LYMPH NODES. THE FEATURES ARE CONSISTENT WITH METASTATIC AMELANOTIC MALIGNANT MELANOMA, HOWEVER, SPECIAL STAINS HAVE BEEN ORDERED TO CONFIRM THE MELANOCYTIC NATURE

Pathology report

Chapter 2

Tracking Back

To understand my healing journey, you will need to know some of my history. On May 7, 1944, twelve years before I was born in a small timber town in the South West of Western Australia, my mother gave birth to a baby girl. Her name was Kathleen Jean, but very sadly, she died at birth. The local doctor and matron were attending an emergency, so Mum was left with a young nurse who had just commenced working at the hospital. Mum was not monitored correctly, and when the doctor returned, he was frantic when he saw that the cord was coming out of the birth canal at the same time as the baby's head. He panicked and tried to push the baby back inside to release the cord. This course of action gave my mum's body shock enough to stop her heart, and the doctor had to tend to her, leaving the baby stuck. By the time he got back to Kathleen, she was dead.

Right up until my mum died at the age of ninety-three, she never recovered from the grief and loss of her first child. She went on to give birth to my brother, Ronald, two years later and my sister, Margaret, three years after that. I wasn't born until seven years after Margaret, so in many ways I felt like an only child, sometimes a replacement child, as I was named Cathryn, which is, of course, very similar to the name Kathleen.

When I was born, my mum told me, the first thing she heard the doctor say was, "Quickly, take the mask off the baby." I was born with a caul over my face. A caul or veil is a thin, filmy membrane that covers a newborn's face and occurs in less than one in eighty thousand births. There is a lot of superstition regarding this phenomenon, but one of the popular European legends suggest that a baby born with a mask like this will have good luck and be protected from drowning. It is also believed that a child born with a caul may be "born with a calling."

When I was a young child, I didn't know about my sister Kathleen, until one day when I was talking to Mum about the death of another baby in the community. She opened up and told me of her experience. This was my first recollection of talking about death, and I remember feeling heavyhearted. Whenever there was any reference to Kathleen, it was always "Mum's baby" with a very deep feeling of grief. I didn't know her name until I was married at twenty-two and obtained a full birth certificate. There it was, listed under the section for names of siblings—Kathleen Jean (deceased).

Mum's birthday was on May 9, two days after the birth and death of Kathleen and she told me how she and her mum sat together in the hospital ward. As they looked out of the window, they saw my father, my grandfather, and the undertaker, walking away with the tiny coffin. They hadn't discussed with my mum where to bury the baby, and she never asked about what they had done with her newborn's body. Our family lived in this timber town for a further twelve years, and still Mum never visited or asked about Kathleen's grave. Her grief was deep and profound.

I know Mum loved me and would do anything for me, but she was such a worrier and this constant anxiety made me fear life and what might happen to *me*. I had to stay safe. Mum couldn't bear the thought of losing another child. This is a common response from parents who have lost a child. As a parent now, I understand why she was overprotective of her children, but as a child, it scared me to know that the world was so dangerous. There were constant warnings of what I couldn't do and should be afraid of in life. I was very overprotected.

There is a term for this now—"helicopter parenting"—because such parents are always hovering above their children. I remember in my twenties waking up in bed one night with Mum shining a torch directly into my face. I jumped and asked, "What are you doing?"

She replied, "Just checking that you were still breathing?"

Really?

She was a good mum, and I do not wish to criticise her, as I know that parents do the best they can with the wisdom and knowledge they have at that time, but Mum's constant fear was really over the top and made me fear life!

When I had my second child, Hayden, everything during the pregnancy went well. At thirty-five weeks, I went to the obstetrician's clinic for a check-up. The nurse asked me to wait while she found the doctor. After examining Hayden, he told me that the baby's heartbeat was rapid, and he was referring me to another doctor, a specialist at a major women's hospital in Perth.

I spent all day there having tests and waiting and then more tests and waiting. I asked a nurse who this doctor was, and she replied, "He is the doctor all the other doctors send their too hard cases to."

Her words made me anxious. I fretted the time away in a stark waiting room until late afternoon before the specialist returned to speak to me. He had called in several other specialists for a meeting to decide what would be the best treatment for my baby. He came straight from that discussion to say, "I'm really sorry, Mrs Brown. I don't know what to do for you."

I was devastated.

The doctors believed that my best option was to be admitted to hospital and receive a drug called digoxin to slow my heartbeat and, hopefully, slow the baby's heart.

Once I was admitted to the hospital and settled into a room, I remember looking out the window and seeing my father-in-law and mother-in-law walking away from the hospital with my daughter,

Carolyn, who was two and a half. I started crying. I was traumatised with fear about what was happening to my baby. And I felt hauntingly alone. The nurses were great, but it was one of those times in my life when there was nothing anyone could say that could pacify me.

By six o'clock, there were a lot of medical staff fussing around, and when one of the nurses came to tend to me, I asked what was going on.

She replied, "Hasn't anyone told you? You are having an emergency caesarean."

I asked, "When?"

"They are waiting in the theatre for you now," she told me.

Panic set in. Bob didn't even know I was in hospital. Mobile phones weren't yet on the scene, so I asked if I could use a telephone to contact him. When he wasn't at home, I rang my parents-in-law; he had just arrived at their place to pick up Carolyn. I told him to come to the hospital ASAP, as it was an hour's drive away.

I felt so exposed and vulnerable as I was prepared for surgery. I remember the anaesthetist asking if I wanted to be "knocked out" or have an epidural. I chose an epidural, as I was terrified my baby would die, and I wouldn't have a chance to hold him if he only lived for a short time.

Thirteen medical staff members were in the operating theatre, all gowned up and ready to see this unusual event. I hardly recognised Bob when he arrived, also wearing a gown. I was very relieved to have him with me.

At 8:11 p.m., as soon as Hayden was born, the doctor quickly showed him to me and then rushed him to ICU. One of the nurses took a Polaroid photo of him and bought it back to me while the doctors stitched me up. I appreciated and treasured this photo. With all this happening, I went into shock and was wrapped up in heated rugs to keep me warm and calm me down. This cherished picture of Hayden gave me something positive to focus on, as I felt my baby had been taken from me, and I felt empty.

Bob stayed with me until 11:00 p.m., while I settled back into the ward. As I started to doze off to sleep at 1:00 a.m., the door flung open, and the light was turned on. In walked three people—a doctor and two nurses. The treatment they had given Hayden to slow his heartbeat wasn't working, and his heart was beating faster than the equipment could measure. They informed me that, if his heart rate didn't slow down in the next hour or so, he would be transferred to the children's hospital and given shock treatment to stabilise his heart. The doctor asked me to call Bob, as it wasn't clear whether our baby would survive the night.

In disbelief, I phoned and woke Bob, asking if he had told Carolyn she had a brother. When he said no, I asked him not to tell her before he had contacted me again in the morning, just in case there was bad news.

My body went back into shock, and my mind started spinning. The nurses wrapped me up in warm rugs again in an attempt to settle me down. I had never felt such emotional pain before. *Not my baby. Not my beautiful baby boy. Please don't let anything happen to him.* I was devastated. I felt hopeless and helpless at not being able to be with my baby. I knew he was being well cared for by the best medical staff, but he must be feeling frightened and alone in ICU.

The night was long, and I looked longingly for the first rays of sunshine through the window. I was never really religious, but I remember praying to God and asking for my baby to be kept safe. I knew it was no good bargaining by saying I'd go to church each Sunday if he could live, but I did promise I would be a good mum and do the very best I could to look after him. As soon as one of the nurses came into my room, I enquired about Hayden. His heartbeat had normalised, but it was expected that he would remain in ICU for some time.

I was very grateful when the nurse transferred me to a wheelchair and wheeled me to the "Special Nursery" to visit him. I wasn't prepared for what I was about to see.

There was my beautiful baby in an incubator and connected by tubes and wires to machines that were flashing, blinking, and making all sorts of strange noises. A nurse was monitoring him continuously. My heart ached to pick him up and give him a cuddle and welcome him into the world. With all the wires strategically placed to keep him safe, all I could do was put my hand through the opening and touch his tiny body. I spoke gently to him, reassuring him that I loved him and that I would always be there for him. I stayed with him for as long as I could to reassure him he was not alone.

Over the next twenty-four hours, many tests were carried out. However, no abnormalities were detected. Thank goodness! When the doctor came to see me again, he said how lucky I was that my original doctor had detected the rapid heartbeat and acted immediately, as usually in cases like this, it was left too long and those babies were stillborn.

After two weeks in intensive care, I was relieved to take Hayden home. I felt extremely grateful for such a good outcome. I had to administer him a very small dose of digoxin every day for twelve months, just to make sure his heartbeat stabilised.

After that terrible crisis, life carried on as normal for six months until one night I was woken up by Hayden struggling to breathe. Bob and I rushed him to the local hospital, where he was diagnosed with severe croup, and we were advised to take him directly to a larger hospital, three quarters of an hour away.

Halfway through the drive to the hospital, Hayden couldn't breathe, and he was physically making the motions of climbing, as if he was trying to come up for air after being under water. We were hoping to find a policeman who could escort us. That didn't happen, but we finally arrived at the hospital, where we stayed for two weeks until Hayden's croup finally subsided enough for him to breathe normally.

Once again, life carried on normally for another six months until, just before Hayden's first birthday, I woke up to the sound of Hayden struggling to breathe and the familiar "barking" sound of croup. We bypassed the local hospital this time and went straight to the larger hospital, which was further away.

When they assessed him, the doctors weren't confident enough to treat him, so they called for an ICU doctor and nurse to come from the major children's hospital in an ambulance to escort Hayden back. He was so small, I had to lie down on the trolley with him strapped to me, and off we went with the sirens of the ambulance screaming as we wove in and out of the traffic, which stopped to let us through.

When we finally arrived, Hayden was examined, and the doctor marked his throat ready for an incision, in case he had to be intubated. If his throat swelled any further, it would stop his breathing. Fortunately, the doctors managed to get tubes through his nose and down his throat before it closed over.

Every couple of hours, the nurses would come and suck the mucous out of these tubes. Hayden was terrified by this procedure and screamed. As his throat was swollen it was an anguished, silent scream. Giant tears flowed from his eyes, which pleaded with me to make the nurses stop. I was overwhelmingly distressed. One part of me just wanted to pick him up to protect him and run from the hospital, but then there was the other logical part that knew, if I did this, he couldn't survive. I remember thinking *I wish it were me and not him*. If I could have taken the pain and suffering away from him, I would have. I never left his side during the day, and at night, I slept in an adjoining room.

*   *   *

I was in a great deal of emotional fear and pain one night when I looked out of the hospital window and noticed a bottle shop. Although I didn't ordinarily drink alcohol, the thought crossed my mind to buy a bottle of brandy and drink until I had plastered all feelings. Thankfully, a more rational part of my brain knew that, if I got drunk and something happened to Hayden during the night,

I would never forgive myself. Not having any other skilful coping strategies, I followed earlier patterns of somehow putting on a brave face and carrying on. Bob would call in after work to see us but he was just as lost as I was.

Hayden had his first birthday in hospital and was a very sick little boy.

At this stage, as we were struggling with our own lives, my sister Margaret was seeing a chiropractor for her sore hip. When the chiropractor asked about her health, she told him our story. He suggested I take Hayden to a particular chiropractor, who, while examining our boy, found two tight areas in his back that were restricting the nerves, one leading to his heart and the other to his throat. It seemed an incredible coincidence that these were the two places he was having health problems. I took Hayden for treatment every month, and he began to thrive.

Once again, our lives settled into a routine, until Hayden was two and a half years old. Bob and I had just dropped Carolyn off at my parents' place for a couple of nights and, on the way home, called into a playground for Hayden to play. I lifted him out of his car seat, and as Bob and I walked off, he ran after us. He fell over, cried, and refused to stand up. Bob picked him up and placed him onto the playground rocking horse to help stop him crying. Hayden howled even louder and wanted me to carry him.

When we got home, he wouldn't get out of the car and walk. I carried him to his bedroom and lay him on his bed to undress him ready for a bath. He let out a piercing cry when I touched his leg. When I looked, I could see it was really swollen and out of shape. We took him immediately to the local hospital, where he was X-rayed and transferred to another hospital yet again.

Hayden had broken his left femur, and as the doctor examined his leg, he unexpectedly pulled it back into alignment (without anaesthetic). Hayden let out a blood-curdling scream with the pain. This upset him further. I started to cry and moved away so Hayden couldn't see me. This distressed him more. I quickly composed myself and sat with him while the doctor put a splint on his leg. I was told he would stay in hospital for six weeks. At this age, children's bones are changing from being flexible to becoming more rigid and can break quite easily.

Keeping a two year old flat on his back, with his leg tied up to a frame, is no easy feat. The ropes holding the leg frame went up over the top of the bed to some heavy lead weights behind the bed's head. Hayden got so frustrated one day, he was thrashing around and his hands found the rope above his head. He gave it a good tug and the lead weights holding his leg extended and straight jumped over the bed's head and landed heavily on his forehead. He let out an almighty shriek, which bought all the nurses running in. They called a doctor from emergency for an examination to ensure that Hayden didn't have a concussion. He was okay but had a huge lump on his forehead. A nurse then found some string and tied the rope to the frame so it wouldn't happen again. By this time, the pressure had me at my wits end.

After two weeks of hospital, I became more and more anxious and again would not leave Hayden's bedside. To add to our anxiety, a door had been left open in one of the other babies' wards, and an older child had walked in and pulled a baby nearby off the bed. I needed to be with Hayden to protect him, but I was also worried about leaving Carolyn again. Although she was getting used to me disappearing for a couple of weeks at a time, and I knew she was safe, I was missing her a lot. In the end, I asked the hospital if I could take Hayden home early.

After much consultation between medical staff, I was allowed to take him home. I set up my lounge as a hospital room and nursed him there for another four weeks.

I thought that was enough for anyone to bear, until two weeks after the frame was removed from his leg, Hayden ended up in hospital again with croup. My heart ached for him, and I wanted to protect him from all this pain and suffering. I was stressed and also felt I was living on "red alert" all the time. Scared and not knowing what was going to happen next, I supposed all the fear and warnings I had received from my mum about life being unsafe were true.

Hayden and Carolyn

CHAPTER 3

Is There Another Way?

I thought I was lost, so I set out on a journey to find myself. What I found was that I wasn't really lost at all, I was just looking in the wrong places. Look in the right places and you will be amazed at what you find.

—Dr. Gary Jackson

Determined to take on fate, I wondered about non-medical support to help me deal with the news I had received from my oncologist. I needed to find another way to deal with my prognosis.

I vividly remember walking into Lee's office. I was very apprehensive, as I had already visited three doctors, and they had given me no help and especially no hope for survival, and so here I was, consulting a naturopath. I noticed immediately the difference in the layout of Lee's office compared with the oncologist's office. The oncologist avoided eye contact with me and had sat as far away from me as he could, jammed on the other side of his large desk. Here was Lee, sitting on my side of the desk, next to me. I felt he was on my side and happy to walk the journey with me. There is a saying—"Your eyes are the window of your soul"—and I felt that, by looking into my eyes, Lee was seeing who I truly was.

Using iridology (diagnosis by examination of the iris of the eye), Lee looked directly into my eyes; and, without any prior knowledge, started telling me the history of my health. He was amazing. It was as if he had my medical records and was reading straight from them. Lee told me that he would not be treating the cancer but was able to help "balance the chemistry" of my body so that my immune system would be strengthened and work well again. I remember him gently tapping me on my leg and saying, "This isn't going to be easy, kid, but we can do it together!"

At first I was a little apprehensive. *Is he just seeing a desperate young mum wanting to be around to see her children grow up, willing to do and pay anything?*

There was something different about Lee. He was honest, positive, encouraging, and very intelligent. *Why would I not trust him?* What were my choices? Three doctors telling me I was going to die or one naturopath who was telling me I could live. I chose Lee, and that was one of the best decisions I have ever made.

He worked out a treatment and eating plan for me, and if it wasn't on my list, I didn't eat it. It was really simple. I would ask myself the question, *Is this food life giving or life taking?* This allowed me to listen to my body and develop my intuition, which began giving me very strong messages of what was right and wrong for me. Nothing passed my lips for two years that wasn't on my list, and my body responded with glowing health. When I met with people who had heard of my cancer diagnosis, their first comment was, "But you look so well."

After the first six weeks of taking herbs, supplements, and other concoctions, I felt terrible. Every muscle in my body ached, a great big lump filled with puss came up in my throat, my breath was foul, and I felt absolutely awful. My first thought was, *Oh no, this isn't working.*

I went back to see Lee, and he was very excited that I felt so bad. *This is fantastic,* he said.

I looked at him quizzically, "Really? Why?"

21

He went on, "Tell me, did you ever have problems with your tonsils as a child?"

My answer was, "Yes. I ended up getting my tonsils out when I was twelve because I was always on antibiotics for tonsillitis."

"And what about your liver?" he persisted.

"Well, when I was five, I had hepatitis A. I had to have six weeks off from school," I replied.

"This is really great. The treatments are working well, and your body is detoxifying. When you start the healing process, it can be like turning time back and going over your whole life. As the hands of time sweep around, they contact and release the energy and toxins of each experience and situation, which may have accumulated in your life. You are now releasing those toxins."

Wow! Was I relieved! When I understood the process, it didn't seem so bad.

As the symptoms cleared up, I felt absolutely fantastic and felt lighter and happier, as if I had let so much go, which is exactly what I had done. Given the right conditions, the body has a remarkable capacity to repair itself.

Through Lee and also through another acquaintance, I heard about the Cancer Support Association of Western Australia, now known as Cancer Support WA. I attended my first meeting the day after my first appointment with Lee. One of the hardest things I have ever had to do is walk up the stairs of the organisation's building and say, "I need help." My stomach was in a knot, and my head was spinning with questions. Also, a question rumbled around inside me, pounding against my resolve: *What can a place like this offer me?*

As it turned out, I was welcomed and embraced by everyone. I was the youngest there by many years, which was also a bit scary. I was fascinated to hear other people talk about their experiences with cancer, physically, mentally, spiritually, and emotionally. I wish I had discovered this place when I'd had my first diagnosis, as Cancer Support WA was so amazing. I was mixing with people who had well and truly outlived their prognoses. They all said, "Listen to the diagnosis and ignore the prognosis. Nobody can tell you how long you have to live. There are so many things you can do to empower yourself."

I was beyond belief that there were so many people willing to support me. Yes, *there is another way!*

Why hadn't the doctors told me about this organisation? They were very busy and could only spend ten to fifteen minutes with me, sending me away to cope with bad news in solitude. It would have been so much easier if one of them had said, "I can't do anything else for you, but why don't you go down to Cancer Support WA. They have people and services there to help you cope with this news."

Unfortunately at that time, I believed oncologists were experts in cancer and knew everything. What I have since discovered is that they are very clever and intelligent people who are trained in treating cancer with mostly chemicals and radiation. I gradually realised that there are many other professional people who are well trained and know how to deal with the mental, emotional, and spiritual aspects of cancer. I found it essential to build my own "healing team." Yes, I did need an oncologist and doctors, but I also needed a support group, a naturopath, reiki, massage, a counsellor, and so on. From where I stand, this isn't a competition on who does it better. Decisions should always be made on what is best for the individual, to help him or her cope and hopefully recover from this multifactorial disease. Everyone is different, and a single combination does not fit all, so each person must develop his or her own healing team. For those who, like me, find that the medical profession can't do any more, at least there are people to offer support mentally, spiritually, and emotionally.

I remember going back to the oncologist and telling him all that I had been doing; I told him about the support groups, the meditation, the nutrition changes I'd made, the counselling, and the reiki—none of them extreme changes, just common-sense lifestyle changes that didn't cost a lot of money. He wasn't the least bit interested. He just ignored me and kept probing my body for tumours. I was confused and couldn't understand why he wasn't interested in what I was doing. I was getting healthier and healthier, and I thought he would be interested and want to know what was happening so he could help others, but sadly, this wasn't the case.

At that time, chest X-rays and physical examinations were the sole measurements of my "progress." I did this every three months for two years. And then at one appointment, the oncologist asked me, "How long was it from the time of your primary to secondary melanoma?"

I replied, "Ten months."

He then said, "How long ago was that?"

I replied, "Two years."

He said in an emotionless voice, "I have no need to see you anymore."

I thought, *Oh well, I'll just get on with what I am doing. He told me I had two months to two years to live, so I suppose, if I'm strong and healthy, I'm a bit of an embarrassment to him and his belief system.*

So I gathered my bag and stood up to leave the room, and just as I had my hand on the door handle, he said, "By the way, don't think that it is anything you have done. There are such things as spontaneous remissions."

I was absolutely flabbergasted. He didn't have a single word of encouragement or acknowledgement of all that I had done on my healing journey. I didn't need his approval, so I walked out of his office and shut the door behind me. I shut the door on this part of my cancer journey and felt as though I was once again free to live my life—free from judgement and negativity.

*   *   *

Six years after my diagnosis, there was an article about me in the newspaper promoting the services at Cancer Support WA, so I decided to write a letter to the oncologist to let him know I was still alive and healthy.

I wrote:

> You may not remember me, but I was your patient in 1990 when I was first diagnosed with melanoma.
>
> I wanted to send you a copy of the article from Monday's *West Australian*, as I hope you will be interested to learn that I am still alive and that I now work with cancer patients. I also want to give you some feedback that may assist you when dealing with cancer patients.
>
> I work directly with approximately fifty cancer patients per week through support groups and wellness programs, and I get a lot of feedback about how what the oncologist says has an enormous effect on the well-being and attitude of the patient.
>
> I remember quite clearly, as if it were yesterday, the words you said to me, i.e. "You are in the hands of fate, and you may live for two months or two years."
>
> Those words were like a bomb and completely shattered my life for the next few months.
>
> I suggest that you consider changing what you say when you break this news to people.
>
> If you had said, "There is nothing the medical profession can do to help you, but you know that many people have helped themselves and improved their quality of life by learning life skills such as meditation and attending cancer support groups," it would have saved me a lot of heartache and devastation. Also when giving a prognosis you could say, "Well some people die very quickly from this disease, and some live to a ripe old age

and die of other causes." It would have been more helpful and hopeful. What cancer patients need is understanding, caring and hope, not a cold clinical response. It would help so much if oncologists would understand this.

I hope you take the above in good faith, as that is how it is intended. I only wish to help others through this very difficult time and try to ease their journey.

Much to his credit, my former oncologist did reply six weeks later, saying he was pleased to hear that I was on top of my malignancy. He explained that it is extremely difficult to know whether or not to give information to patients and that, sometimes, communication fails. He wished me all the best for the future and hoped that I could help others who experienced similar difficulties.

These few words of encouragement meant the world to me. Perhaps this oncologist will now be more mindful of the way he imparts bad news to others. I hope I am not coming across as critical of oncologists. I am only telling my story as I experienced it, but after working with thousands of people over several decades, I have continuously heard from people in my groups who are more distressed about the way they have been emotionally and mentally treated than they are about the diagnosis of cancer. There must be a better way of delivering such bad news—a way that doesn't strip people of hope. This is true for all health professionals, whatever their healing modality. Hope is a very important component in the recovery from cancer or any other life-threatening disease. If you don't have hope, you are only left with despair and a feeling of hopelessness and helplessness. Mentally and emotionally, that is a death sentence.

Both Lee and Cancer Support WA told me about Balya Cancer Retreat. I wasn't sure exactly what this entailed but decided that I had to try everything. The retreat was run by a doctor, and she had several facilitators come in and talk about the many and varied aspects of the cancer journey. One volunteer was doing reiki, and as I had never heard about it before, I asked for a session. The practitioner placed one hand on my wrist and one on my shoulder. I felt gentle energy flowing through my arm where I'd had the surgery.

She touched more than my arm; she also touched my soul. It became apparent to me that this journey was now about discovering who I was, and I had to find out more. Cancer was the catalyst that awakened a sleeping giant inside me—my soul. I realised there was so much more to overcoming cancer than I was initially aware of. I was slowly awakening to something much, much bigger than me—my soul's journey.

I was fascinated by one of the presenters, Nigel, who talked about the Silva Method of Mind Control. His message to all of us was that it is the mind that chooses everything you do. So if your mind isn't clear and focussed, your life isn't clear and focussed. I hung on every word he said, and this also led me onto a journey of discovering just how powerful the mind is when we learn to master it and not be a slave to it.

I remember Nigel asking the room of thirty cancer patients, "How many of you want to live to be a hundred?" We all shot our arms up. And then he said, "Do you still want to live to be a hundred if your partner has died?" A few people put their hands down. "Do you still want to live to one hundred if one of your children has died?" More hands went down. "Do you still want to live to a hundred if you don't have any money?" More hands went down. And finally, "Do you still want to live to a hundred if you are dribbling and incontinent?" There was lots of laughter, and lots of hands went down.

His message was this: Life isn't conditional. You have to decide to live life and take on all its challenges. I decided, *Yes, I do want life!* And I decided that I was ready for the challenge to discover who I really was and what my mind was capable of.

The great philosopher Joseph Campbell said, "The warrior's

approach is to say 'yes' to life: say 'yea' to it all. Participate joyfully in the sorrows of the world. We cannot cure the world of sorrows, but we can choose to live in joy. When we talk about settling the world's problems, we're barking up the wrong tree. The world is perfect. It's a mess. It has always been a mess. We are not going to change it. Our job is to straighten out our own lives."

At the conclusion of the retreat, one of the exercises was to write a letter to your "self," to make a connection to your soul, to write a script for your life.

This is what I wrote, blissfully unaware of what I was really doing:

> Dear Self,
> Well here we are after this wonderful weekend. We are going to have such fun together and express love to each other and to many, many others.
> My life has to have contact with people, and if I can help them in any way, I will be joyous in this knowledge.
> We will laugh, love, and live together in total harmony. In this faith, opportunities will be directed to us that we cannot at this point of time envisage, and I know from deep down that they will come.
> Travelling to all corners of the earth will be part of our journey together. Abundance will follow us, and our needs at all times will be met. I know our example will encourage others to nurture this relationship and that they need to go within and make contact. It is our right to have all of these things, and nothing is going to deny long life to enjoy these visions.
>
> With love,
> Cathy

It was at this time that I knew I had to change my mind and let go of fear. I had to surrender and trust the process of life, allowing my soul's journey to unfold in divine order, not my order. There is a saying that says: "If you always do what you have always done, you will always get what you have always got." If I needed my life to change, I needed to change my mind, and that is exactly what I did.

I had travelled fairly extensively before having children, and I had always wanted to take my kids overseas. I wanted to teach them to be brave and release fear, and I wanted to show them what a wonderful world we live in. I wanted them to accept, celebrate, and embrace people from all cultures, as this was what made us all unique and individual.

To make these wishes come true, I had to release my fears and start taking chances, so I booked and paid for the family to go to Bali in twelve months' time. I know people thought I was crazy, as I had been given only two years at the most to live, but I needed something positive in the future to focus on. I was also giving my subconscious mind the message that I intended to be around in twelve months' time.

I also received the renewal for my driver's license about the same time. Now there was a dilemma. Was I to renew it for twelve months or should I renew it for five years? I gave this great consideration and eventually came to the conclusion that, if I took it out for only twelve months, I was admitting that I didn't think I would be around for five years. Urged on by the Scottish blood inherited from my grandmother, I paid for five years and decided I was going to get my money's worth! I had made up my mind that I was going to live my life as though I was going to live forever.

My sister-in-law Sanchia came to visit me just after I returned home from hospital. It was one of those days when I was having some "what if" thoughts. *What if I'm fooling myself? What if this doesn't work? What if I die?*

Sanchia lived in the country, so this was the first time I had seen her since my diagnosis. I opened the front door to find her standing there. We just hugged each other tightly and cried together. We were good mates and had shared a lot of experiences together. I told her that I wished I could live at least another five years. I just wanted to see the kids that little bit older and independent. She only stayed for a short time, as she was on her way to see a psychic.

Two hours later, there was very loud and urgent knocking on my front door. I opened it up to find Sanchia standing there. She was beaming with excitement. Apparently the psychic had said to her, "There is someone close in your life who has just been diagnosed with cancer. Ask her why she only wants five years more. Tell her to set her mind on fifty years."

We were both very excited at this possibility. How on earth had this psychic picked up something so specific? There is so much more to this world than we can see.

On another occasion, I was walking around the Fremantle Markets when I saw a poster about palmistry. I was standing looking at it when a man came out and said, "You're next," assuming I was waiting for him. My first instinct was to say, "No, I'm not interested. Thank you." But something else was louder in my head and said, "Yes."

So in I went, not knowing what I was doing there. He asked to look at my palm. He started off by saying things that anyone could guess like, "You are married. You have two children." He then looked at my hand intently and looked directly up at me and said, "Your health hasn't been too good, has it?" I didn't want to give anything away, so I just shrugged my shoulders in a non-committal way. He then leant forward and quietly said, "I am not allowed to predict life, but there is life after thirty-five if you want it."

Wow. I was thirty-three, and the oncologist had said I had two months to two years. That would make me thirty-five, if I survived to his longest prognosis for me. So there was the question directly in front of me. *Do I want life after thirty-five?*

The answer was an unfaltering, *Yes! Of course I do!*

I made up my mind there and then that I would do whatever

it took to survive and live to a ripe old age. I have family members who'd lived into their late eighties and nineties. I reasoned with myself that I had the genetics and potential to live just as long myself. I just needed to create the right conditions for my body to heal. It was as though there were messages everywhere directing me toward my destiny. I made a choice to live and decided to follow my intuition, surrendering and allowing it to lead me to wherever I needed to go to meet my destiny.

I also very vividly remember being asked the question at a seminar. "Do you want an ordinary life or an extraordinary life?" I remember wholeheartedly deciding then and there that I wanted life, an extraordinary life. I didn't just want to survive cancer; I wanted to thrive.

CHAPTER 4

Reiki

After having a very positive reiki experience at the Balya Retreat, I had a deep desire to know more about this healing modality. I asked around within my local community to find further information. The Internet was not yet at everyone's fingertips in those days, so finding reliable resources was challenging. Reiki was very new to Australia, so accessing information was very difficult.

In the meantime, Mavis, a friend of mine, had been going to a Spiritualist church and asked if I would like to join her. This concept was new to me, and I had no idea what to expect, but I was desperate for any help and felt that I had nothing to lose. A group of approximately thirty people met in a small local hall every Tuesday night, where they would meditate and give feedback on their experience. At the end of the meeting, I was invited to move to the middle of the circle and sit on a chair. The group would surround me and project healing energy my way. I was overwhelmed by their care and compassion and found this procedure absolutely amazing. The sensation felt like they were all pouring a warm and nurturing substance through the top of my head, and as it cascaded down through my body, there was a profound feeling of being embraced by love. There was also a deep sense of relaxation and peace after having this type of healing. It certainly was very special.

Mavis spoke of a woman, Jackie, who had recently learnt reiki and asked if she was willing to see me. Jackie's answer was, "Yes, I've been waiting for her." Apparently in her meditation, Jackie (who is psychic) was told a young woman with cancer who had two young children would be coming to see her. She had also heard others in our small community talking about me but didn't know how to make contact.

I phoned her and subsequently visited her home every day for a week and, on some occasions, would be there for three hours! When I arrived at the house, I would lie on a massage table fully clothed, and Jackie and her husband Jim would place their healing hands on my body. During this time, I could feel waves of soothing warmth from their hands flow through my body. Many times I fell asleep as I relaxed and absorbed this unique experience. They were both wonderful people and very kind to me.

Jackie also ran spiritual development courses. I decided to join the group, as I had a deep yearning to discover more. Exploring this subject took me out of my comfort zone, as I had been brought up as a Methodist until I was sixteen and then worked for the Anglican Church for nine years. What I discovered about myself was that I accelerated my personal growth when I chose to be open-minded about new subjects.

One night, the group was meeting in a seminar room adjacent to a complex in which a group of men with disabilities were living. One of the men wandered in and asked what we were doing, so Jackie invited him to join us. He went on to explain that he had been in an accident many years earlier and, as a result, had a steel plate inserted in his skull. His mother was a well-known psychic in England but had died many years previously, leaving him alone. We all felt very sorry for the man and so welcomed him into our group for the evening.

After an hour of stimulating discussion regarding spiritual development, it was time for us to meditate. Jim stood up to dim the lights, and as the soft music entered my ears, Jackie's soothing voice guided me into deep relaxation.

After ten minutes, I heard someone moving. I opened my eyes slightly to see what was happening and was very surprised to see the man coming straight toward me. I froze, not knowing how to respond. My heart was racing as he stood in front of me and gently placed his hands on my head. Immediately, I felt the most amazing surge of energy fill my body. This warmth was strangely familiar as it was being absorbed into every cell, muscle, tendon, and bone of my body. I relaxed into my chair and the experience, simply allowing it to happen. I experienced no fear and no judgement; I just merged into the moment, feeling safe and secure. Why I responded like this, I do not consciously know, but I think it was because I was aware that Jackie and Jim were alert and watching the man's every move. There was a knowing from within the group that this man was not going to hurt me. Time stood still during this experience, but I imagine it lasted about ten minutes, and when he was finished, he calmly turned around and sat down.

Jim immediately turned the lights back on, and when everyone was settled, Jackie asked the man what had drawn him to place his hands on my head and not on anyone else. He replied that, while he was meditating, his mother had come to him and told him to place his hands on my head so I could have a healing. He was simply doing what he had been told to do!

That experience given to me by a stranger challenged all my core beliefs! I didn't understand any of this stuff. All I knew was that I felt fantastic, and I was intrigued. What happened reinforced in me the belief that, if I didn't have an open mind, I would miss out on many important and unseen aspects of life. I had depended too strongly on my sense of sight to understand the world, but this highlighted to me the importance of developing my other senses. I released all judgement and realised that, when I judged others, I was only reinforcing my own limited beliefs and experiences of life. There is a saying, "Your mind is like a parachute; it only works when it is open." Life had unexpectedly pushed me out of the plane. My mind was now open, and I was flying.

I decided to learn reiki so that I could self-heal and release my dependence on others. In May 1991, I attended a seminar facilitated by Beth Gray, a reiki master who travelled from the United States of America each year teaching reiki all around Australia.

When she arrived in Perth, sixty people attended her seminar at the Fremantle Maritime Museum, a solid building that contained much atmosphere and history. We were divided into groups of ten and led into a small room, where Beth would perform a ceremony to "tune" us into reiki. Beth had a beautiful pink rose in the room, which shared its exquisite perfume with us all. As she moved along the line to each person, I sat patiently with my eyes closed, waiting for my turn. My senses drank in this exquisite experience. I was aware of Beth's location because her bracelet sounded like tiny bells tinkling in the distance.

When it was finally my turn, Beth placed my hands in the prayer position and started to do something above my head. My hands started to shake uncontrollably, and my body buzzed. I felt like I had been plugged into a very powerful electrical socket. When she was finished, Beth asked everyone to stand up and leave, but I was unable to stand as my body was still shaking. I wasn't frightened. Just fascinated that something like this was happening to me.

Beth wasn't concerned; she asked a couple of men to assist me back to my seat. These men stood on either side of me, linked their arms into mine, and guided me back into the main room

When Sanchia saw me shaking uncontrollably, she was shocked. She commented, "We brought you here with cancer, and now we are taking you home with cancer and uncontrollable shaking!" We both laughed, as we were unsure how else to respond to this unusual situation.

Every subsequent time I performed reiki, my hands shook uncontrollably and warmth built within me as though I was in a sauna. The energy surged through my body and into the person I was "treating." Given the incredible intensity I experienced, I was reluctant to place my hands on anyone.

Six months later, Beth returned, and I booked in to learn the next level, Reiki II. I told her about the shaking and how it was getting stronger and stronger. She instructed me to say silently in my mind, *Treat this person like a delicate china cup.* I would try it at the first opportunity and discover, much to my amazement, that the shaking slowed down.

Another woman came and whispered into my ear, "You shouldn't be restricting this energy. You should be developing it."

After the seminar, this same woman suggested that I should meet Carol at the Seekers Centre in Subiaco. The Seekers Centre was a place for people to meet to develop their psychic abilities. I hadn't heard of it previously.

After explaining my concerns about the shaking, Carol asked me to place my hands on her. I hesitated, as by this time the energy was just about knocking people over. She then told me to place my hands approximately twenty centimetres above her body, and the most incredible thing happened. My hands began to move of their own accord—flapping and moving around uncontrollably. I could feel the energy around her body. It reminded me of clouds in the sky. Some of the energy felt like it was heavy and dark, and then it would change to light and flowing. My eyes just about popped out of my head. *This isn't me. I'm not doing this stuff!* I would never have considered myself "New Age," and here I was flapping my arms around this woman without any control over what was happening.

Carol explained to me that when I was attuned into reiki, it not only opened up my ability to channel reiki energy, it also opened up another form of healing. I explained to her that this just wasn't my "thing," and she reassured me and said that only people who needed this type of healing would come to me, and she was right. In all my years of practising, I have never had anyone ask me to stop. On the contrary, I have had a very positive response to this healing modality, which I include in the "energy sessions" I do for people.

In 1996, I decided to become a reiki teacher, also known as a reiki master, so that I could share this wonderful gift with others. A very dear friend of mine Beverley, who was already a reiki master, took me to another level of understanding and development of my spiritual self.

I have noticed that, when people are first diagnosed with cancer, their first focus is usually on the physical—changing their diet, exercising, making sure they get plenty of rest. This is all very important, but I believe that, although they are harder to grasp, the spiritual, mental, and emotional aspects of our being are just as important. It is my belief that this is where the key to cancer recovery lies for some people.

Since Richard Nixon declared war on cancer, it is estimated that billions of dollars have been spent on searching for a cure. Most research has looked in the physical body for the cause of cancer. This may be the place to look for some cancers, but not all. What if the answer isn't in the physical body? What if it lies within the spiritual, mental, or emotional aspects of who we are? True healing comes from within, from finding peace in the heart through forgiveness, peace in the mind through meditation, and peace in the soul by finding purpose. Everyone's healing journey is unique. Every individual must explore deeper into his or her life's journey, looking beyond the obvious and outside the boundaries of limiting beliefs.

Mine was not to be an easy journey, but it has certainly been an extremely rewarding one. I discovered that "there are many pathways up the mountain." I have taught reiki for years and have witnessed many "healings." Reiki isn't secret, but it is very sacred, and I know that, when people take the time to create "sacred" time in their lives, miracles can happen. A whole new world of understanding and possibility opens up.

From my experiences, reiki is personal and experiential. Reiki taught me to have "sacred" time in my life, a time to just be. Meditation and reiki are wonderful tools for creating this space. Discovering the "spiritual self" is different for everyone. Some find it through organised religion, some through meditation, some through reiki, and others by being connected to nature. Deep down, we are all seeking the same thing—a need to be connected and loved. Learning to celebrate and embrace the differences in religious preferences would certainly go a long way toward healing the world of conflict. The world is not a bad place. Without judgement and anger, we would be left with a world filled with peace and love.

Each person has the responsibility to heal him or herself and find his or her own inner peace. Our individual inner peace affects the people around us, and so the "body of humankind" will slowly heal one cell (person) at a time. If you find yourself judging this statement, simply ask yourself why you feel like this. Keep asking yourself questions. You only get answers when you ask questions. Any toxic thoughts or feelings that you hold inside your own mind/body toward other people are not hurting them; they are destroying you.

People often ask me what I did to heal. These people are usually looking for a "magic pill" to take without much effort on their behalf, but unfortunately, there isn't a "magic pill." Tumours and illness are the symptoms of disease. You can cut, burn, and poison them out, but if the conditions don't change, nothing else changes. Some people don't want to hear this, and that is their choice. I will not force my beliefs or experiences on anyone. However, I would like to share with those who are both open and interested that there is another way. Healing takes time. Examining toxic thoughts, feelings, and emotions and releasing them is a critical element of the process.

Scientists acknowledge that only a very small proportion of our mind is utilised—the conscious section of our mind. What lurks within the subconscious? Very few people are brave enough to explore. They may discover things they didn't want to know. Perhaps finding out about past lives will shake up their beliefs. What would their lives look like then? Having the desire to reconnect to the "true self," the unconditional love, and the stillness and light that is within everyone is a great focus for the mind. It is this spark that we call life. When it leaves our body, we die.

Reiki is performed by "laying on hands" and is based on the idea that there is an unseen life force energy flowing through us, and this is what causes us to be alive. I often smile to myself when I am sitting with my hands on someone giving reiki and recall the oncologist saying to me, "You're in the hands of fate." He should have said, "Your life is in your hands."

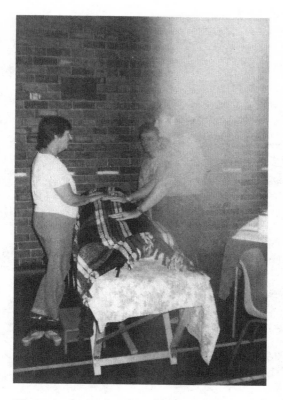

Giving reiki with white light all around me

39

CHAPTER 5

The Healing Journey

The Wanslea building, which houses Cancer Support WA, is a heritage building built over a hundred years ago as an orphanage and, with its high, pressed metal ceilings, is a stunning example of the architecture of that era. The people of Western Australia are very lucky that it is still available for the community to utilise. When I first attended Cancer Support WA, I was encouraged to have some counselling, although I wasn't sure what the benefit would be. The counselling room I was shown into was dark, with a small lamp warmly glowing in the corner. After sitting down, I remember looking up at the ceiling and finding myself intrigued with the interlocking patterns embossed into the tin. There were small intricate patterns melding into each other, creating larger patterns. Life can be like this, smaller intricate experiences being part of the larger "big picture."

I was sitting there anxiously, and a little apprehensively, talking with the counsellor, when he suddenly said to me, "What is the worst thing that has ever happened to you?"

He explained that research is now showing that long-term stress can be a contributing factor to suppressing the immune system and impacting health. This type of stress can also lead to people feeling a sense of hopelessness and helplessness.

Out came the story of my fears from when Hayden was a baby and the time when he was in hospital. "He was very sick and the doctor had inserted a tube to help him breath. As the tubes filled up with mucus, a nurse would come and turn on another machine, which sucked and cleared the fluids from the tube. These tubes were going in through his nose and down through his throat, so when he cried, no noise would escape from his voice box. There was a look of terror on his face when he heard the machine start up, and huge tears would fall from his eyes; he was terrified. I would do all that I could to comfort and reassure him that everything would be okay. I remember looking at him and thinking, *I wish it were me, not you, going through this.* As a mum, my heart ached for him. I didn't want him to suffer. I wanted to protect him by picking him up and running out of the hospital, but I knew if I did this, he could die. All I could do was hold him and try to comfort him. This ate away at me and ripped me apart inside. Wanting to protect Hayden but knowing I couldn't do anything made me feel totally hopeless and helpless as a mother—disempowered to make decisions about someone I adored and was responsible for, my baby."

I then went on to tell the counsellor about my mum losing her first baby. When I finished my story, he sat there for some time reflecting in silence. I was confused by his response and not sure whether I had upset him or whether or not I should continue talking. After much contemplation, he simply said to me, "If you die before your child, you won't have to live your life with the trauma and grief your mother has."

Wow! This hit somewhere deep inside and shifted my thinking. Every hair on the back of my neck and arms stood up straight. There was a "dead" feeling in my stomach, and it started to twist and churn. *Is this the truth? Could I have had a death wish deep in my subconscious mind without even being aware of it? How could this be? I had a fantastic life. I had everything I wanted. So much to live for!*

There is much that we don't understand about the mind and what it remembers. It is a powerful and driving factor in our lives.

I have learned that we aren't always aware of what is buried deep down in the subconscious mind, and sometimes it takes a "crisis" for this to rise to the surface for healing. Is this why we get sick? To bring our awareness to unconscious beliefs, emotions, and memories of past experiences that need resolving and expression? This theory might not be for everyone, but by my body's response, it certainly was true for me.

I devoured every book I could find about healing, trying to discover more about the subconscious mind and beliefs. Many books made reference to *You Can Heal Your Life* by Louise Hayes. I thought I would research this book one day but never got around to it. Other books I wanted to read just kept piling up by the side of my bed, waiting patiently for my attention.

Word had spread through my children's school regarding my diagnosis with cancer. My daughter's friend came to play after school one day, and when her mother, Julie, came to pick her up, she asked me if I knew a woman called Robin from the school.

"No, I don't know a Robin," I replied.

Julie placed a book on my kitchen bench, and there it was—*You Can Heal Your Life* by Louise Hay. An inscription inside read, "Just another concept for you, Cathy. Love Robin."

I was incredibly moved that someone who didn't know me had gone to this much trouble, and here, right in front of me, was the book I had been wanting to get hold of. The universe has many ways of gaining your attention, and this was one of those times for me. I read the book from cover to cover, and it gave me a deeper insight into my mind. It was just what I was searching for. This was a revelation and explained how thoughts and emotions manifest disease in the body. I savoured and contemplated every challenging concept. This book truly expanded my mind to all sorts of healing possibilities.

Sometime later, I remember lying on a massage table in the lounge room of my home with two friends graciously giving me reiki. My body started to go icy cold and felt strange inside. I started squirming and wriggling around, trying to make myself more comfortable. My friends were both becoming concerned with my behaviour and one of them said to me, "Cath, where are you?"

My first logical thought was, *I'm in my lounge room.* But a second later, the focus changed, and I began to cry and shake like I was going into shock. I was so very cold; a deep icy feeling had pervaded my body. I was a frightened baby, lying alone on a cold, stainless steel bench. I cried out aloud from somewhere deep within my being, *I'm not dead. I'm still alive. Can't you see me? Please don't abandon me. Please don't leave me here.*

I was frantic, not knowing where these thoughts, feelings, and emotions were coming from, and in a strange way, I was floating above the scene. It became crystal clear. Not like a dream. It was real. There was my mum lying on a bed, with the doctor tending to her, frantically trying to restart her heart. The young nurse was fussing around, and there was my tiny body, cold and rejected, lying on a cold, stainless steel bench, abandoned by everyone, not even noticed. As I relived this scene, my body shook as I cried and released emotions trapped in a deep cavern within my mind, a place that I had never visited before. My mind was swirling around from confused thoughts to thoughts of disbelief that this had just happened to me. I tried to make some sense of what I was experiencing.

What is happening now? *Am I losing my mind?* I felt a rush of pent-up energy leave my body. The energy felt like a deep sadness, or grief, escaping from a place it had been trapped. I had never known my life without this energy, and now I was in a very deep place of stillness and peace. This sensation reminded me of a warm rug being tenderly wrapped around my body, keeping me safe and warm.

This is one experience my mind still has trouble categorising and making sense of. I don't entirely understand how the mind works, but I am becoming more and more convinced about past lives. *Was I my mother's first baby Kathleen? Did I carry the experience deep within my being? Was this my way of releasing the grief I had been conceived in?*

Thoughts, thoughts, and more thoughts again came, confusing

43

me. There were more questions than answers, but one thing is certain; this experience has changed my life. I don't know if it is even possible for our rational minds to make sense of an experience like this. I had to go deeper, beyond the obvious, to a place that is not often explored. It is a place of trust in something bigger than me, a place where it doesn't need to make sense to the conscious mind.

I am not asking for anyone to believe me or make judgement about my experiences in life. I am telling my story openly and with honesty, sharing with you how my life has unfolded and how I am integrating this knowledge. Some people will go through their whole life without ever having unusual experiences, but I have found that, when I share this story with people, they often open up and tell me their own incredible experiences. For me, it is a great honour that they trust me enough to share. Usually they then go on to tell me they have not shared such information with anyone else previously, for fear of being mocked and judged. I think it is sad when people are ridiculed by others who don't understand or have never had such deep life experiences.

For a short time, I pondered whether I would share my experiences but then decided that it would not be fair to tell half the story and not the whole story of my healing journey. Hopefully it will show open-minded people another way when they are feeling trapped, with nowhere else to go.

After this experience, I also read Shirley MacLaine's books. I adored her honesty as she explained the exceptional experiences she'd had in life by travelling to exotic places and meeting amazing people. I was reading *Out on a Limb* in bed one night, and I turned to my husband and said, "I don't know how I am going to do it but I want to set foot on as many continents as I can and have amazing experiences like this before I die." He grunted, rolled over, and went to sleep, obviously not interested in a life like that. We had done a fair bit of travelling as a family when the children were young, and it is my love of travel and adventure that fuels my passion for life.

I was regularly attending the Cancer Support WA support group and felt inspired by interacting with people going through similar circumstances. We all inspired each other and loved encouraging new members to be proactive in their search for wellness. There was never any judgement about peoples' choices, just openness and acceptance.

Volunteering as a telephone counsellor, visiting people in hospital, giving presentations to schools and Rotary Clubs defined a tangible sense of purpose in my life. I instigated and organised a reiki clinic at Cancer Support WA that proved very popular with the members and was a wonderful way to expand peoples' perception of healing.

After I'd been doing this voluntary work for five years, the support group facilitator, Lisa, asked me if I would facilitate the group for three months while she took a long service leave. I felt honoured to be asked but, at the same time, was uncertain of my capabilities. After many talks and much encouragement from members of the board and Lisa, I agreed to run the group, as well as facilitate the twelve-week wellness course while she was away. I loved every minute of this challenge and felt that I had finally found my calling.

Much to my surprise, Lisa phoned me at the end of her long service leave to inform me that she had resigned and asked me to take the job on permanently. *Me?* This had come out of left field. I felt humbled to be offered this job, however, although I had five years of experience within support groups, I did not have any qualifications. I knew that I had developed many skills through personal involvement and experience but now realised that, if I wanted to pursue this as a career, I needed formal qualifications.

After doing substantial research into course offerings, I booked myself into a two-year, group facilitation course at the Wasley Institute, a training centre for this type of work in Perth. This ended up being one of the best professional and personal development courses I have ever attended. Tom, who facilitated the training, extended me past my perceived limits every week. His philosophy?

"If you are not prepared to face your own fears, how can you expect to be there for people while you are facilitating a group? You need to be confident within yourself to create a place of safety for others."

I successfully completed this professional training program in group work leadership. I was extremely grateful for the excellent supervision I received along the path toward my development as a group facilitator from very skilled people.

During the interviewing process to be accepted into this training, Tom asked me why I wanted to do this work. I told him I felt that it was where I needed to be—my calling. He enquired whether I had any experience, and when he asked me this, it reminded me of a time when I was nineteen and asked by the director of Anglican Health and Welfare to go and work with him so he could train me up as a counsellor. I refused his request, as I felt I was much too young to be working with people in this way.

Hearing my story, Tom responded, "Isn't life amazing. This opportunity has come full circle and is asking you the question again. Are you ready this time?"

My answer was a definite, "Yes."

When I was first diagnosed, reading Dr. Ian Gawler's *You Can Conquer Cancer* was a revelation to me, and I couldn't put it down. I devoured the information in this book and found it to be a wonderful compass to guide me through the initial hurdles of my healing journey. Through his own personal journey with osteosarcoma, Ian has collected and shared much knowledge, making it easy for others to feel it is possible for them to make a difference in their experience with cancer. My first introduction to meditation was when I lay on my lounge room floor, listening to his tape. I was trying to teach myself to meditate and to integrate the principles of healing that I had read about in his book.

As further training for my new role, I was now being sent to the Yarra Valley on the other side of Australia, to be trained by Ian to run the twelve-week wellness course, based on that very book. I was very excited and enjoyed being involved in the whole experience. The

Yarra Valley is a beautiful part of the world, and being inspired by Ian and meeting up with a whole group of like-minded people fed a yearning in my soul. I found kindred spirits who thought like me, ate what I ate, and loved meditating, in a beautiful natural setting. I thought I had gone to heaven! This couldn't possibly be part of my work! I have been told that the richest people in the world don't work a day in their lives; they just get paid to do what they love. Well, that was me. I had found my "calling," and my life felt extremely rich on all levels.

I immersed myself in this work for another six years and absolutely thrived. Expanding the use of my newly developed skills, I instigated a women's healing circle, an open support group in Rockingham, and facilitated the volunteer carer's support meetings. Life at Cancer Support WA proved very rewarding—that was until we came under new management.

After a couple of months of attempting to make a difference in a new, reorganised setting, I knew that this wasn't the right place for me, and it was time to move on to the next phase of my working life. There was a knowing that I needed to grow, explore other avenues, and expand my knowledge. Some of my colleagues felt the same way, and three therapeutic staff resigned the same day. I felt saddened to make this decision, as Cancer Support WA had been a lifeline for me. But after ten years with the organisation, I felt another life beckoning.

A friend and I started up a business teaching the principles of wellness to the corporate world. Our aim was to share the knowledge we had gained through our own experiences with people who were still well. We hoped to help them prevent disease by informing them of simple lifestyle changes they could make. This was an enormous challenge, as participants were attending the sessions not because they wanted to but because their employers had sent them. I found this demoralising, as I was accustomed to working with people who were enthusiastic about making positive changes in their lives, and I soon realised that I was in the wrong business.

Reading the newspaper one day, I was attracted to an advertisement regarding hypnotherapy training. I knew immediately that this was the change I had been waiting for—a change in direction that would help me to understand the mind even more. Hypnotherapy, at this time, was in the middle of being deregulated in Western Australia, one of the only states in Australia where, as a prerequisite to practising hypnotherapy, you had to be a doctor, dentist, or psychologist.

Even so, this comprehensive hypnotherapy training was exactly what I needed and opened me up further to the wonders of the mind. Once again, I was excited and thrived in this environment, completing every available course I could find. Over the next four years, my understanding deepened as I attended seminars on advanced mind dynamics, hypnosis as an allied therapy for the improvement in the quality of life for cancer sufferers, and power hypnosis. Finally, I received my Diploma of Clinical Hypnotherapy in 2013.

Hypnosis is a simple yet powerful tool in resolving all sorts of difficulties, and I love working with this healing modality. How people change their lives when they change their perception about their problems never ceases to amaze me. My aim is to empower people to create the happy, healthy, and abundant lives they deserve. I cannot do it for them. I encourage and help them to change their perceptions and, therefore, their minds. I show them another way. Often I tell my clients that I would prefer to be known as a "mind coach," rather than a "clinical hypnotherapist." My role is to coach them on how to tap into the incredible power they have in their own deep, subconscious minds and harness this by changing their beliefs and minds about their perceived difficulties. They do the rest.

As I have said previously, there are many pathways up the mountain when it comes to healing. And people sometimes need help to explore the many aspects of who they are—body, mind, spirit, and emotions—from their "healing team." A tumour is the symptom of a disease, not the cause. It is very important to explore beyond the obvious and break through perceived boundaries. I share my story, not as a blueprint for healing, because there isn't one, but hopefully to inspire people to take control of their health and their lives and break out of self-imposed mind limitations.

CHAPTER 6

Everything Changes

It is not the strongest of the species that survives, nor the most intelligent; it is the one most adaptable to change.

There is some controversy over whether or not Charles Darwin was the author of the quote that begins this chapter, but regardless of who said it, for me, it resonated strongly. My life took so many unexpected twists and turns, I had no choice but to learn to live with uncertainty and become adaptable.

I vividly remember the first time I met Bob. His sister Evadne and I worked together, and she had been trying to set us up together for several months. One Friday night after work, she took me home to meet him. As soon as I saw him walk out of the house to greet us, my heart did a little flutter. As a young girl, all I ever dreamt about was getting married and having children. And here he was, the love of my life, the man of my dreams.

I was only sixteen, and Bob nineteen. He worked in the country and would drive for hours to spend the weekend in Perth with me. We dated for six years before marrying; subsequently built a home; and, after two years, started our family. Life was really good, and I was blissful in this role of wife and mother.

In 1988, I kept a diary. Looking back, it was a very uneventful year. I was a young mum, contentedly bringing up my family and doing the usual things a young mum does. But there is one entry I would like to share with you. It was the conclusion to the diary—Sunday, January 1, 1989. It reads:

> Well, here we are, 1989! What a wonderful year I have had. Writing this diary has been the hardest thing. Sometimes I would forget for a week or two and then have to recall what had happened previously. It made me realise just how quickly time flies and it has helped me realise just what a wonderful life I have and also what wonderful people surround me. I often wonder why I am so lucky to have Bob for my husband and Carolyn and Hayden (two delightful children). It also extends to two kind and loving families from which we have both come. If everyone were surrounded by this type of love, the world would be a better place.

Little did I know what life had in store for me in the years to follow. It was only six months later, in June, that I had the melanoma removed, and then three months later, my father died two weeks after a traffic accident. He and Mum were driving in their car when a fully loaded sand truck went through a red light, smashing into the side of the car and consequently dragging them some distance along the road, trapping Dad in the mangled mess. Mum was helped from the car by strangers before the car caught alight. This was terrifying for everyone concerned, and Dad was very lucky when someone passing by had a fire extinguisher in his car and stopped to extinguish the flames. He was then rescued by the fire brigade with the Jaws of Life, and both Mum and Dad were taken to hospital in an ambulance and treated.

Mum had a broken sternum and was very badly bruised and in shock but was released home that same day. Dad stayed in hospital overnight and returned home the following day. However he still had dried blood on his face and hair from the injuries he'd sustained in the collision. He was in excruciating pain but couldn't articulate exactly where it was, so we called his usual family doctor to come and visit him at home. The doctor suggested that his discomfort was due to internal bruising and reassured him that everything would be okay. We were all shocked when he died a few days later.

Autopsy results stated that he had a neoplasm in his stomach, which had burst, and confirmed he had eleven cracked ribs! Poor Dad. He was a good man and didn't deserve to die like this. A representative from the hospital visited Mum at home, as she was in too much pain to get into a car, and he apologised for the neglect. *How could someone have been released in this state? Wasn't he thoroughly checked? The dried blood had not even been washed from his face and hair!*

It was a situation that could have been taken to court. However, as a family, we decided to focus our attention on Mum and her recovery. Her bruising from the seatbelt was extensive, and her knee had taken a massive blow. Losing her husband of forty-seven years was an enormous shock for her.

It was about this time that Bob's twin sister, Kareece, was diagnosed with breast cancer. She was only thirty-six. This diagnosis was unexpected, as she was fit and healthy and had always looked after herself. She had surgery and chemo and carried on with her life as usual, with dreams that she would be well enough to have a child.

The unexpected reoccurrence of my secondary melanoma was six months after this, so our families were in turmoil. I was frightened. My life was disintegrating around me.

Three years later, Bob's mum was diagnosed with bowel cancer and died. So here he was, dealing with his wife, his twin sister, and his mother all experiencing cancer, all at the same time. Previously, there had been no history of cancer on either side of our families, so with all of the recent news, we were reeling in the shock. Our minds were in overload as we tried to cope and make sense of the situation.

Bob was amazing during this time. With so much uncertainty, the way he held everything together while I was busy on my healing journey was commendable. I could feel that he was becoming emotionally a little distant, but with everything that was happening in our lives, who could blame him? He was diligently focused on work and then, on top of that, focussed on holding our family and everything else together. Bob kept extremely busy. I think he was secretly worried what would happen if he stopped for a moment and allowed himself to feel the turmoil of emotions inside.

Unfortunately, in 1999, Kareece died of secondary breast cancer. It had been a long journey for her, with many ups and downs. By this time, she had given birth to a beautiful baby girl, who'd brought her an abundance of love and joy. That she was leaving behind a three-year-old was heart-wrenching. Life can be so unfair. Grief brought my fears to the surface once again, and I gave my children an extra big hug the night Kareece passed, expressing my gratitude to be alive and to be with them.

Life carried on until we had another huge shock in 2003, when Bob's nephew Sachsa unexpectedly died at the age of twenty-four. We were all devastated that this precious young life had been taken. But nothing could prepare us for the death of Sanchia (mother of Sachsa) only thirteen weeks later. The family was sent spinning and reeling once again from these tragedies. *How could so much gloom descend upon us?* We were emotionally shattered.

At Christmastime I would light a candle with an angel on it for each family member who had died, but this ritual was becoming increasingly harder to face as the cluster of candles grew. I reached a point where I dreaded answering the telephone.

It was at this time I realised that Bob and I were growing further apart. Everything just became too hard, and cracks began to appear in our relationship. I tried to patch them up as best I could, but as I patched one, a crack would appear elsewhere. I tried hard to make it work for the sake of the family, or so I believed. I had invested thirty-six years of my life into this relationship, and at this time, it felt necessary to me that I try to give our marriage a chance to get back on track.

Relationships can be complicated and complex, as they affect not only the two people involved, but also the people around the primary couple. Once the ties are stretched and broken, it is very difficult to put them perfectly back together again. It is like a delicate container that has been shattered. You can glue it back together, but the cracks are always there. To say I was stressed during this time is an understatement. Everything I believed in about marriage, family, love, and life were no longer relevant to me. I questioned everything. As I was questioning my beliefs, I was also searching for a way to reassemble my life. Relationship issues hurt intensely and cut deep within the soul, but I managed to put on a brave face and focus on the future, leaving past hurts behind. It's a bit like driving a car. You have to keep looking forward (in life) through the windscreen so you can see where you are going. If you keep looking in the rear vision mirror (the past), you will crash. I wanted to give "us" the best chance. I was acutely aware of my heightened stress levels and used every resource I had to manage it. A reoccurrence of melanoma was the last thing I needed.

With all this as its background, 2009 was a real doozy. It was the year my life changed direction yet again, and not by choice. The year started off really well, with Hayden marrying Cindy on February 7. It was an emotional day for me as I proudly watched my son standing so tall, strong, and handsome, waiting for his bride. As tears silently slipped down my cheeks, my mind wandered to the time of his birth and the many exciting adventures of him growing up. I pondered the challenges and the joy of raising a son. And here he was now, getting married and starting a family of his own. I remember thinking how proud I was of him and everything he had achieved. He had so much to look forward to, and I was thankful that he was strong and healthy to enjoy it, particularly after the start in life that he endured.

I love both of my children unconditionally, and I will always be there for them if they need me, but I often remind myself, *I gave them life, but I can't live it for them.* It was time for me to let go of them both and allow them to create their own lives.

The following Saturday, Carolyn moved away to live in the United Kingdom for two years. I also vividly recall the day she was married. I cried as she walked down the aisle at Guildford Grammar School Chapel, looking beautiful and confident on the arm of her father. I reluctantly allowed my mind to wander and contemplate how different her life would have been if I had died all those years ago. Imagining how difficult it would have been for her to grow up without her mum to guide her through the important adolescent years. I was extremely grateful and tremendously proud to be alive and witnessing this momentous occasion in her life.

She and her husband, Kevin, are both engineers and love to travel, so it made sense that, when Kevin moved to Cambridge for further studies, Carolyn would follow and work in London. This plan enabled them to realise their dreams together. Saying farewell to her at the airport was both agony and delight. My feelings and emotions were bubbling just beneath the surface. Carolyn made me proud of what she had already achieved in her life. She had achieved many awards at school (head girl in primary school, dux in high school for both years eleven and twelve) and had completed university with a double degree in applied chemistry and chemical engineering. The world was her oyster, and here she was taking advantage of the opportunity to travel and explore. This was the start of her journey of discovery. Paradoxically, I was also feeling sad, as she would be on the other side of the world and I would miss her desperately. Once again, I reminded myself that, although I had given her life, I couldn't live it for her.

I generally don't believe in begging. However, I was desperate to make my marriage work at this time and identified a holiday in the United Kingdom as being a great opportunity to share some quality time with Bob, now that we were free of the responsibilities of parenting and could focus on our relationship. I pleaded with him to come with me and visit Carolyn and Kevin in London, but to no avail. He was not interested and would not compromise on this decision.

After many discussions, I decided that I needed to go anyway, to get away from everything and to think things through. I boarded the plane solo and with a heavy heart, as Bob didn't want to come with me and share this once in a lifetime adventure. Reluctantly, I accepted his decision.

I visited Europe for six weeks and, during this time, explored England and Scotland with Carolyn and travelled to Eastern Europe on an organised tour. I grew a lot during this time, looking at my life from a distance and evaluating everything in my life with new eyes. I viewed things from a different perspective and came to the realisation that I deserved better and that it was up to me to make some really tough decisions.

By the time I arrived home, I knew that my marriage to Bob was over. He had also had time to think things through while I was away, and when I returned, I found him to be cold and distant. After thirty-six years, thirty of them married, I gathered all my courage together and walked out to the back garden where he was sitting under the pergola and told him I couldn't continue. I couldn't live a lie anymore. I couldn't stay in a marriage where we were both unhappy. He didn't respond or react. He just said, "Okay." He was emotionless. We then sat and discussed how we would separate and began the process immediately.

A couple of weeks earlier, while I was in the United Kingdom, my fifteen-year-old dog, Ted, had to be put down. He was a dear little shih-tzu and had been a wonderful companion for me through the troubled years. I was much attached to him and very sad to lose him, but I was getting used to "letting go." What a year of letting go this turned out to be!

Peppered with more unexpected deaths, 2010 was yet another year of tragedy. Brodie, another one of Sanchia's sons, died at the age of thirty-two, leaving behind a wife and two beautiful little girls. And my brother's son, Bradley, died at the age of thirty-four.

I remember Mum ringing me up on August 26, twenty years since Dad had died. She told me that she had some good news and some bad news. Kristen, my sister Margaret's, daughter, had birthed a beautiful baby boy at 8:00 a.m. in the morning, and Bradley had died at 9:00 a.m. of a heart attack, all on the one day. *Slam!* My emotions hit the wall again. It was particularly difficult trying to support Mum through this time, as I was not in an emotional state to support her or anyone else. I was really struggling, coming to terms with my own emotions. It felt like I was emotionally bankrupt—running on empty but still attempting to function and remain engaged in life.

There is something about the order of things and how life should be. Here we were unexpectedly losing our young. Five people under the age of fifty-three, and three of them under thirty-five, had passed. Grief and loss closed in. We were all heartbroken and struggling.

Also at this time, my friend and business partner of ten years and I were also rapidly growing apart. With all that I had been through and was going through, I was unable to meet her expectations at work. I decided that it was time to hand the business over to her and walk away. It was sad, but I intuitively knew that it was something I had to do. My life was changing direction rapidly, and I was uncertain where I would end up. I needed to be free to make decisions about my work and life without restrictions and expectations from anyone.

Our family home of thirty years was sold in November. This forced me to clean out thirty years of memories and possessions. I spent many hours going through cupboards and finding objects that evoked sad emotions and also reminded me of the happy times when our family was together. This was like walking down a twisting and turning pathway, through the many and varied experiences of my life. I had to decide what I was going to keep and what I was willing to let go, and then there was the pile of items I needed more time to decide about. This process was, on both a physical and emotional level, very challenging.

With this chore finally completed, I moved into my mum's beach house. The beach was my solace, my friend, and my comfort—a very special place to reflect. I spent many hours swimming, walking, and sitting on the beach, contemplating my future and watching the mood of the ocean change as the weather conditions changed around it.

It really was my *annus horribilis* (a Latin phrase meaning "horrible year"), and I was acutely aware that I had to take care of myself, as I had learned years earlier that long-term stress was not good for my health. It seemed that everything I had been attached to or responsible for, had been "released"—family, home, work, relationships—some happily and others tragically. I was completely free of commitments. My life seemed to have a force of its own beyond my control and was rapidly changing. Having no idea what to do with my life now, I decided creating a new life, the happy, healthy and abundant life that I deserved, was the best option. I needed time to figure out how I would manage all of this change and uncertainty. My life certainly was unfolding, but I had no idea in which direction it was going.

It was at this time that I started my own business—Life XL. This name reflected my new focus. I wanted to excel (XL) in life and I also wanted an "extra large" (extraordinary) life.

CHAPTER 7

Rock Bottom

The beach house I moved into after my home was sold was originally owned by my parents, but after Dad died, it became neglected and run-down. It was very basic, but it was a safe haven for me to retreat to while I re-evaluated my life. In some ways, this house reflected who I had become—run-down, neglected, and needing much work to restore it to its full potential. Even the rust eating away at the gutters under the paint reminded me of the cancer that had been eating away at me many years ago.

My first night there was horrendous. I was alone, with nowhere to hide from my pain and feeling the full effects of my emotions. They were like hot molten lava, spewing up from deep within a volcano—no longer contained or able to be managed. So I just surrendered to their power and allowed them to express themselves with tears, rapid breathing, and sobs of despair. I didn't know where to put myself. Everywhere I went, my pain followed.

What will become of me? What will I do? Why did this happen to me? The questions just kept coming again and again; I had no answers. *Go away questions! I don't want to think. I don't want to feel.* I was beside myself with pain. It was at this time that I reached a very deep part of my soul and decided that the only thing I could do was surrender to whatever life had in store for me in this lifetime. Stress and anxiety comes from trying to change what is happening, and on this night, I decided to surrender and observe, to finally let go and allow my soul to guide me, and to discover what my "soul contract" was in this lifetime. This was the night my ego died.

The rain was pouring down a couple of days later, and I recall pulling into the driveway feeling miserable. Without thinking, I automatically put my hand in the glove box of the car, looking for the remote control for the garage door. When I couldn't find it, I burst out laughing. For many years, I had become accustomed to the "mod cons" in my previous home, and now I was back to basics. This incident made me realise how much of a rut I had been in and how mindless I had become. I opened the car door, ran through the persistent rain, unlocked the garage door, and reminded myself to show gratitude when I finally installed a remote for the garage door. I needed to become mindful and live in the moment, not in the past or in the future—to live my life with gratitude.

The Thursday night after I moved into my new abode, the reality hit me hard again. Once again, I drove into the garage after a day out, and as I sat there, ready to turn off the ignition, a song came on the radio. It was "Call the Man" by Celine Dion, in which she croons about calling the man "who deals in love beyond repair." I turned the music up as loudly as my ears could cope with and cried and sobbed, releasing another wave of emotion. The song finished with a drum beating loudly like a heartbeat and then faded away. The silence it left was deafening. I felt completely empty and alone. I prayed for someone to heal my broken heart, to take the excruciating pain away. As I walked into the house, it felt so empty that nothing seemed familiar. Desperate to have company, I lit a candle. This ritual helped me feel as though there was a silent presence in the room, witnessing my journey, but I couldn't settle to do anything. I needed to be connected with people, so I decided to walk down the road to a small hall where the Spiritualist church was holding a meeting that night.

I hadn't been to a Spiritualist church for years and didn't really know anyone in the room, except the woman running the meeting. As I walked in, I saw there was a door raffle, so I decided to buy five tickets. The room was sparse, with only a few chairs set out for the people attending and a small table at the front, covered with a white tablecloth and a small vase of flowers, which looked like someone had picked them from their garden. There was also a table on the side, full of unwrapped prizes, ready for the raffle draw. I had been to these meetings a few times previously but had never received a "message from beyond the veil."

One of the mediums stood up, commenced the session, and immediately looked straight to me and said, "I see a photo of an older man—perhaps your grandfather—walking in Forrest Place in Perth?" She continued to give me a detailed description of the man. I didn't know either of my grandfathers. They'd both died before I was born, but this description matched a photo my mum had of her father, so I accepted the suggestion. She continued, "He has been watching over you for some time, as you have been very stressed and worried about your future. He wants to let you know that he is proud of you and that everything will turn out all right."

I know I was upset and vulnerable, but hearing these words gave me much comfort and hope. I could feel my inner strength returning.

At the end of the evening, it was time to announce the winners of the raffle. Many tickets were drawn, and people rushed up to the raffle table and thoughtfully selected a prize. One of my tickets was drawn. I reluctantly walked up to the table to select a prize. I didn't really need anything as I had just shifted house and had intentionally cleared my space of knick-knacks that overfilled my cupboards. Not wanting to offend anyone, I scanned the prizes offered. Nothing caught my attention or attracted me until, out of the corner of my eye, I saw an unwrapped and unmarked box on the edge of the table. I don't know why I chose this, but it had the element of intrigue and surprise, as there were no markings on the side.

Staying for a cuppa afterward was more than I could handle

this evening. I didn't feel like making small talk, so I quietly slipped out and walked home alone through the dimly lit streets, dreading entering an empty house again. When I arrived home, I sat and stared at the unmarked box for some time, contemplating whether I would open it tonight or leave it for another time or perhaps even wait until Christmas, which was only a few weeks away.

After some consideration, I decided to open the parcel. I couldn't believe my eyes. There was the most beautiful hand-carved, wooden angel. She was tall and stylish, with her delicate hands touching and holding her exposed heart—a beautiful, pink heart that was whole and complete, skilfully carved on her chest. An angel had been sent to mend my broken heart, just like I had prayed for earlier in the evening. I closed my eyes and held her to my chest. My heart was thumping, and I welcomed her as a "sign" that things would get better for me. Faith and hope are powerful healers, and at this stage, this was all that I had.

CHAPTER 8

Findhorn: Expect a Miracle

It was 4:00 p.m. on a Sunday when Bob and I had agreed to end our marriage. The next twenty-four hours were horrendous. *What have I done? Am I doing the right thing?* Even though I know I am making the right decision, I am in absolute turmoil. *What will I do? Where will I go? How do I support myself financially? How do I support myself emotionally?* My whole life and everything I believe in are no longer true for me. *Who am I really? Why am I here on Earth? What is life all about? Who can I trust?* I felt exhausted, disconnected, and overwhelmed. I was so lost.

I cried, surrendered, and prayed to a power or force greater than myself again. "I don't know why I am on this earth, but please show me what I am supposed to be doing. I am lost and feel very alone. Nothing makes sense to me anymore, and I just don't know what to do."

At 4:00 p.m. on the following day, I received a telephone call from Geoff, a former colleague who was managing the twelve-week Gawler Foundation Course at Cancer Support WA, which I had facilitated for six years prior. He told me that it was time for him to move on in his life and that Dr. Ian Gawler had asked him to phone me to see whether I was interested in taking it over again.

You have got to be kidding me! I hadn't heard from anyone from

Cancer Support WA for ten years and then, out of the blue, I receive a phone call like this. This timing was unbelievable. Obviously my answer was, "Yes."

I contacted Ian, and he invited me to join him in the Yarra Valley for some further training and a refresh of my skills. Here I was again, back at the Gawler Foundation, surrounded by supportive people and returning to a place of healing—the first steps of a journey to a new and better life. I had no idea where life was going to take me. I had *surrendered,* and now I had to learn to *trust* a force greater than myself.

After much research and reading, I have developed a belief that works really well for me. I believe that we have "sacred" or "spiritual contracts." The people and experiences we have in our lives are there for a reason. They are to guide us back to realising who we truly are—a powerful spiritual being having a human experience. I decided to take ownership for how I responded to the experiences in my life.

I know beyond doubt that everything that happened in my life didn't happen to make me a victim, it happened so that I would grow and learn about the incredible power I have inside me. Everyone has this power but, unfortunately, people look outside of themselves and to other people for answers. What I discovered was that all my answers are within. My ego life had to be released so that my soul could be free from beliefs that no longer worked for me. My life needed to unfold in a way that would allow me to follow my calling and honour my spiritual contract.

Carolyn and Kevin were still living in the United Kingdom at this time, so I decided to return for another six-week holiday. Every tour I tried to book into didn't eventuate. Nothing was falling into place, and there was a sense of being blocked. I was frustrated and just about ready to hand it all over to Carolyn and say, "Book me into whatever you can," when I woke bolt upright at 2:00 a.m. one morning and thought, *I'm going to go to Findhorn.*

All I knew about Findhorn was that it was a spiritual community, recognised by the United Nations as having one of the most environmentally friendly and eco sustainable ways of living and looking after the earth. I didn't know exactly where Findhorn was or what I would find there. Over the years, I had heard people talk about their experiences, and this must have planted the seed in my mind.

Half sleepy, I jumped out of bed and researched where Findhorn was and how to get there. I couldn't believe what I found. Two weeks previously, I'd had a visit from friends who lived in Aberdeen, Scotland, and they had invited me to stay with them. I'd declined their very generous offer, explaining that I had already been to Scotland twice, many years ago when I was twenty years old and also the previous year when Carolyn and I had hired a car to explore the Highlands and the Isle of Skye. Sharing this time with Carolyn had been wonderful; we were two women on an adventure, tracing our ancestors in Largs, a small coastal village not far from Glasgow. I felt very privileged to be able to spend this time with her as an adult, both of us with a passion for travel and adventure.

Now, right in front of me on my computer screen were the directions. The way to get to Findhorn was through Aberdeen! A smile developed on my face. *Can this be a coincidence or is there a bigger plan for me?* I hastily sent Thelma and Raymond an email to revoke my initial decline of their very generous offer to stay with them, and they were delighted.

The next day, I received a telephone call from them saying they were very excited that I was going to Scotland and that they would love to pick me up from the airport. They had already planned for me to stay with them for a couple of days so that we could explore Aberdeen together. They would then drive me the two hours to Findhorn, which was near the small town of Forres, and come back a week later to collect me. I would then spend another night with them before they returned me to the airport, ready to fly to Ireland.

Wow, door-to-door service! I was overwhelmed with their generosity. It was as though the universe had bought them into my life to help me get to Findhorn. With this sort of support, I decided to apply for a "Findhorn Experience." As part of the application process, the foundation asks you to send an email, saying why you wanted to go and what your spiritual experience was. I sent this off and applied for August 7, my birthday. This was the gift I was giving to myself, and there were rumblings of excitement and anticipation deep inside me.

Amazing is the only word I can use to explain how the rest of my holiday now effortlessly fell into place. As if by magic, I discovered a tour around Ireland that started from Dublin on the Wednesday after I left Scotland, returning the following Wednesday, in time for me to catch a ferry and train back to London, just in time for a long weekend in Paris with Carolyn.

I was very excited and happy to be going to Findhorn, even though I didn't really know much about the place. Trusting my intuition was new and exciting. I was telling the members of my wellness group about my impending travel plans when one of the ladies offered to loan me a couple of books about Findhorn. She promised to post them to me so that I could read them before I left. Three days later, I had just finished a hypnotherapy session with a client at home when she started telling me about her dream of going to Findhorn one day. I was amazed that she'd started talking about Findhorn without any prompting from me. When she finished her story, I told her that I would be there in a months' time. The doorbell rang while we were talking, and I excused myself to answer the door. It was a courier delivering the books about Findhorn! What a coincidence. Findhorn signposts were all around me.

It was with great anticipation that I boarded the plane, very excited that I was going to see Carolyn again and also fascinated and intrigued about my attraction to Findhorn, a place I knew very little about. After a couple of days rest in London, I flew to Aberdeen.

Scotland is a beautiful country. Driving to Findhorn, I was sitting in the backseat of the car admiring the countryside when I started to get very strong feelings of "going home" and mentioned this to Raymond and Thelma. Even though we discussed this feeling of mine, we could not come up with a logical explanation for it.

Arriving at Findhorn, Raymond insisted on checking the place out with me. I walked through the door into the reception area, and immediately the woman behind the desk looked up and said, "Welcome back. It is so lovely to see you again."

Stunned, I swung around to see if anyone was behind me. No, no one was there. I replied, "I've never been here before. This is my first time."

She apologised and explained, "It's just that you look very familiar, and I feel as though I know you."

As my eyes scanned the room, nothing looked familiar, but the feelings inside of me were relaying that everything was familiar and safe. I experienced a deep and comforting sense of coming home.

Findhorn's motto is "expect a miracle." I didn't go there expecting anything. I was going to find myself and heal. I needed a sanctuary, a safe place to contemplate my life, rest, and decide upon my ambitions for the future. I couldn't have selected a better place for this.

I dragged my suitcase up the stairs to the room that I would be sharing with other women, one Spanish and two German. After lunch it was time to meet the rest of the group that I would spend the following seven days with. There were twenty-four people from all around the world.

After the introductions, the group went on a tour of the Cluny Hill College, where we were staying. Cluny Hill College is owned by Findhorn and is a one hundred-room former Victorian spa nestled in the forests of Cluny Hill. The building is large, imposing, and surrounded by gardens lovingly nurtured by the people who live there. Dinner was set out in a large dining room. Our group table had been decorated for my birthday, and I was particularly surprised when a birthday cake was produced. I felt embarrassed by all the fuss but touched by the gesture. The Brazilian facilitator, Rhonna, encouraged me to sit back and celebrate *who you are.* This was very difficult for me because I had lost "myself" and didn't know who I truly was or how to celebrate "me." My purpose of coming here was to explore and find myself again.

Sunday found the group being directed to the ballroom for sacred dance. I had no idea what we would be doing. However, I found it to be fun and a wonderful opportunity to connect with the other people in the group. I connected with Jim, a Scotsman who is now living in South Africa. He is a biomedical researcher and had just won the European Literary Award for his book, *Deeper than Colour*. We had spoken briefly the night previously when he'd mentioned something about my home town, Perth, Western Australia, in his introduction. My ears had pricked up, as I hadn't expected anyone to know about Perth, and I'd enquired what he knew about it. Jim's son lived there. Conversation carried on, and then I asked if he had any other children.

He said, "Yes, two sons in South Africa, and a daughter in London."

Amazingly, we each had a son living in Perth and a daughter living in Richmond, London.

After lunch, we went on the bus to "the Park" for a tour. This is the original site of Findhorn, where Eileen and Peter Caddy, along with Dorothy Maclean, started this spiritual community. The original caravan they lived in still stands there today, nestled among the eclectic buildings that surround it.

In the evening, we were allocated chores for the week. "Work is love in action" is a quote that is freely used to encourage people to become engaged and part of the process. Our group members meditated, and displayed on the walls around the room were posters indicating how many people were required to work in each department. I felt strongly drawn to the kitchen. I wasn't sure why but just knew that it was where I wanted to be. The process was intriguing, as most of the departments attracted exactly the required number of people. There were only two departments where too many people congregated, so it was skilfully negotiated for a few of them to move to their second choice.

Arriving in the large kitchen, those of us who'd been drawn to the kitchen introduced ourselves to members of other groups who were also participating. We were encouraged to express how we were feeling and then focused our attention on "connecting" to the "kitchen angel" to help us prepare the food. This procedure simply entailed sitting still and reflecting on why we were there, which was to prepare food with love to nourish people. Richard, the team leader, spoke about the kitchen being the "Heart of Cluny" and it being our job to fill the food with love. I found this concept very interesting; I had come to Findhorn to mend my broken heart, and here I was in the Heart of Cluny, the perfect place for me.

I was feeling a flow of energy through my body, wave after wave of tingling warmth that made the hair on the back of my neck stand up. It also felt as though someone was playing with the hair on the top of my head. I have had some strange experiences in my life, but I had never encountered anything like this. The only way I can describe this process was that it felt as though something was stirring and awakening inside of me.

After the work shift was over, I sat down and decided that I needed to go and find the "power point". One of the permanent residents had told me that the power point was a small hill located in the forest, next to the building, and is considered an earth power point (energy lay line). Two other Australian women, Diane and Kerry, asked if they could join me. So the three Aussie ladies set off to explore the surrounding area and find the power point.

As we walked there, I discovered Diane was psychic and a minister in the Spiritualist church. She was going to a psychic conference at St. Andrew's Golf Course after her time at Findhorn. Now there was an unusual combination, golf and psychic development! By coincidence, I discovered that Kerry had gone to school with a friend of mine in country New South Wales. What a small world.

When we arrived at the top of the hill, the three of us explored where the energy was most powerful and then stood in a circle holding hands and meditated. Wow, I'm not sure what happened next, but the power of the energy started to surge through me even more powerfully. I was shaking and swaying around, just like I had when I'd learnt reiki twenty years earlier. I was thankful I had Diane and Kerry supporting and holding onto me. Diane started talking and encouraging me. I can't remember everything she said, as I was crying and releasing very painful, deep, and powerful emotions, but I do remember that she was saying to let the energy flow as I had "work to do on earth." I wasn't sure what this meant, so I just surrendered to the experience and allowed it to have full expression.

The feeling of "coming home" intensified, but I was confused, as I was also torn between thoughts of staying or leaving. I wasn't sure what this meant and felt bewildered and overwhelmed with these thoughts, feelings and emotions rushing through me.

Why do I tell you this story? Because this experience transformed my life, and I will never forget the power that I felt on this particular day. I ended up sobbing with these two special women hugging and holding onto me. I was very grateful that they were with me to share this magical and mystical place—two strangers and yet perfect guides for my healing journey. We must have looked a sight together, but as luck would have it, no one else came near to disturb us or interrupt this experience. Nothing was arranged or orchestrated. The process had a life of its own and unfolded naturally.

The following day, our group was playing "discovery games" in the ballroom. These were wonderful games of mirroring, holding each others' hands with our eyes closed, guessing, and discovering who we were with. There was also a game of trust, where after pairing up, the person in front closed his or her eyes while the person behind guided his or her partner safely through the crowd. Jim and I were partners. For some inexplicable reason, I trusted him entirely, which was an interesting response, given that he was a total stranger to me.

With this experiment in trust complete, we moved to the next scheduled exercise. People were asked to choose a partner, and everyone paired up together, leaving Jim and myself the only two people leftover, standing alone on opposite sides of the room. There was much laughter when we joked about being "left over" and subsequently partnered again. This "unfolding exercise" was one of the most profound activities that we did.

One partner was asked to lie on a mat on the ground, curled in the foetal position on his or her side. With soft music playing, the other person was then instructed to gently and lovingly move his or her partner's arms and legs, unfolding the body. Symbolically, we were unfolding and opening people up to discover who they truly were and discovering a deeper spiritual meaning to life. Jim was the first to lie down. I gently moved his arms and legs, unfolding him and rolling him over on his back, stretching his body out; unfolding him energetically and reminding him on a deeper, subconscious level of the great spiritual being he was. It was an honour to perform such a ritual for another person. As he lay quietly in this position, I had no idea what was happening in his mind.

We were instructed to swap positions, and now it was my turn to lie on the mat, tightly curled up with Jim kneeling beside me on the ground. He was instructed to gently unfold my arms and legs, stretching out my body. I was very relaxed and aware physically but surprised by my inner feelings and thoughts. Something very strange was happening to me; my inner world began to churn and swirl around. I was acutely aware of a sensation of heavy fog and confusion lifting. My path was unfolding, and I was rediscovering a part of myself that had been missing for a long time. It was a profound moment. Energetically, everything was released, and I was exactly where I needed to be. What a journey of self-discovery. Simultaneously, I felt as though my soul had been nourished and my heart healed. Everything I had experienced in my life had been leading me to this moment. The feelings of expansion and a rush of unconditional love for life cascaded through me. Not only did I want life, I reaffirmed that I wanted an exceptional life. The only way I was ever going to create this life was to release the pain, grief, and betrayal of the past. Everything crystallised, and it was then that I realised I am 100 per cent in charge of how I responded to my life. My life wasn't about what happened to me but how I responded to it. I had no control over other people or events, only my response.

I love the Proust quote, "We don't receive wisdom; we must discover it for ourselves after a journey that no one can take for us or spare us."

CHAPTER 9

The Reconnection

Tuesday, day three of my "Findhorn experience" found me back in the kitchen after morning meditation and breakfast. Team leader Michaela set me on my task for the day. The temperature wasn't particularly warm, but I found myself feeling hot, and I was feeling waves of energy surging through my body once again. *Is it just me?*

Michaela looked up with beads of perspiration on her face and said that she was having an energy surge. I told her that I was too. Other people in the kitchen seemed fine. Michaela was very sensitive to energy, and she added that, on the previous night, there had been a new moon and there was a very powerful line-up of planets, which only happens every two hundred to three hundred years.

I had no knowledge of astronomy or the effects of planets upon us but felt fortunate to be in Findhorn at this time. I explained my experience at the power point to her. She was very interested and said that the earth energy was very powerful at this point and that many people came to Findhorn to heal and make sense of their lives. *How did I know to come here to learn to love, trust, and heal? Was it my intuition, angels, spirit guides, inner knowing?* I honestly didn't know. I was just grateful that I had taken the chance and listened to that little voice inside me. I would never have believed any of this was possible before I'd had cancer. What I realised was that cancer, for me, was the pathway back to reconnecting to my soul.

During the afternoon, the group went on an outing to Randolph's Leap, a scenic, beautiful spot in Moray where the River Findhorn is squeezed through narrow rocks. I spent most of my time here with Diane, as she was teaching me how to "feel and sense" energy. She was very generous with her time, and I found it fascinating and most interesting that someone with this gift was so willing to share her knowledge with me.

That evening after dinner, we had a guest speaker. This man had been a part of the Findhorn community for thirty years, and he was telling us how he had come for a couple of weeks but felt that he needed to stay longer. Apparently, this happens to many people when they visit. The evening was particularly enjoyable, and he concluded by singing a funny song, which delighted everyone in attendance.

His talk got me thinking, and I realised I had the choice to simplify my life or complicate it unnecessarily. This reminded me of a banner I had seen in the streets of Perth years ago, which stated, "Live simply, so you can simply live." What a great message.

Wednesday morning was a group project. No kitchen duties today. We were all decked out with yellow weatherproofs and large Wellington boots. What a sight—twenty-four people dressed to go to "the Field," a community based project growing organic vegetables.

The rain was heavy and continuous when we alighted the bus. There in front of us was a very large field of cabbages, which had to be weeded by hand, as no chemicals were allowed. Hoes were issued to each of us, and we set off to contribute to this worthy project. *I hoe, I hoe, it's off to work we go,* was silently repeating in my head as I marched toward the cabbages. Thick, gluggy mud was sticking to my boots, making the pathway very slippery. Surprisingly, even though the rain was bucketing down and leaking through my raincoat, I was having the time of my life. A small group of us worked together as a team and chatted about our unusual experiences as we worked our way down the long rows of cabbages. The conversation was stimulating, and the two and a half hours just flew by. Every row we completed, we grew taller and taller, and heavier and heavier, as the mud stuck to the bottom of our boots.

Hot tea and biscuits were served in a tiny shed where we gathered afterward, dripping, muddy, and exhausted from the work. Some people who lived in the centre of Rome and Paris had disliked the experience and felt angry that they were asked to work in such conditions. I told them how I'd loved every moment of it and had found the experience most invigorating, as I'd reconnected back to nature and the earth. They hadn't thought about it from that perspective and were willing to be a little more tolerant of the situation. Many years ago, I read a book that suggested that the further you were away from nature the more at dis-ease you were. I was very connected on this day, mud and all.

On our way back to the Park, the leader pointed out a rock on the side of the road in Forres that commemorated where the witches had been killed and burnt centuries ago. The inscription on the rock says, "Witches Stone. From Cluny Hill witches were rolled in stout barrels through which spikes were driven. Where the barrels stopped they were burned with their mangled contents. This stone marks the site of one such burning."

Throughout the week, I kept getting stronger and stronger feelings about this history. Images were flashing in my mind of the "witches and wise ones" being slaughtered because of their wisdom and knowledge. They weren't images of cartoon witches that have been made popular in the last century, wizened old hags wearing black, pointy hats and cackling madly. They were images of "crones," the wise women who were persecuted because they understood life. They worked with the natural cycles of death and renewal. These very wise women understood that, without death, release, and letting go, there can be no renewal and fresh starts. They worked with the cycles of nature, not against them, and this frightened people who didn't understand. What a tragedy that so many were killed because of the ignorance of others. Today in our society, these women would be midwives, herbalists, and naturopaths.

Images of innocent women being forced into stout barrels with spikes jammed through them, bleeding and distressed as the barrels were pushed down the hill, haunted me. Feelings of anger rose within me when I thought about their mangled bodies being burnt at the bottom of the hill, with the perpetrators lighting the fire and standing triumphantly and smugly smiling over the contorted mess. These feelings were very strong, and I couldn't understand my obsession with them.

Could I have been involved in any way with these Crones in a Past Life? Have I come back to forgive, remember, and reconnect back to this knowledge

Many years previously, I'd had many moles removed (before I had cancer), and I'd commented that I looked like I'd been stabbed all over. Was the mystery of the bullous pemphigoid blisters on my legs remnants of this life? Was I reconnecting to something deep from within my soul? Was the energy that surged through my body when I gave Reiki a reminder of this time? Or were these feelings and images just echoes from a past time or a way for my mind to resolve trauma?

So many questions swarmed through my mind, and once again there were not enough answers. *Is this experience real or my imagination? What is real in this world?*

These experiences happened and were real to me and perhaps they were another way of healing and a reawakening of forgotten knowledge. All I know for sure is that I came away from Findhorn a dramatically different person. How could my life change so drastically in just one week?

Friday morning, it was back to the kitchen for the last time for more feeding of the soul. I had felt so depleted and spiritually hungry for such a long time, but now I was feeling nourished and satisfied. While we finished the preparation of food in the kitchen, we participated in a ceremony of disconnecting from the "kitchen angel," who we had asked to help us prepare food for everyone with love that would nourish those who ate on all levels. It was during one of these ceremonies I realised that, at home, the only room in which I didn't have an angel was my kitchen, and I was going to rectify this when I returned to Australia.

Seven days had passed so quickly, yet so much had happened in this time. As a farewell, on the final night, we were asked to bring something of ourselves to depict our "Experience Week." Some sang, some did a meditation, others played CDs, and I decided to write a poem:

> I started on my journey
> Heavy in my heart.
> The love I found in Findhorn
> Has given me a new start.
> Everyone is special,
> And I would like you all to know
> That without your contribution,
> I would not know where to go.
> Some have touched me very deeply.
> This took me by surprise.
> And on my lifetime journey,
> I'll carry with great pride,
> The love and gratitude I feel,
> For all of you inside.
> Our time together has come to an end,
> And sadness we must feel,
> But just remember deep inside,
> It was the angels who helped you heal.
> So now it is with lots of pride
> That we return to our lives and seek
> As far better people for having participated in the
> Findhorn Experience Week.

After breakfast on the last morning, we hugged and said goodbye. That twenty-four strangers from all around the world could come together and love and support each in one week is, in itself, a miracle. Each person had amazing experiences—his or her own journey back to inner peace and wholeness.

As I said goodbye to Jim, I told him that I wanted to create a place like Findhorn in Perth—a sanctuary, a place of healing—and I wanted to travel around the world exploring "spiritual" places like Findhorn, not just the usual tourist thing of flashing through big cities with a camera on a whirlwind visit. My perspective on life and travel had changed.

While I was waiting for Raymond and Thelma to collect me, I was talking to Dominique, a woman from Paris who I had become friends with. I told her that I was going to walk down to see the witches' stone in Forres before I left. I needed to get some resolution to the feelings I had been experiencing. The hair on her arms stood up when I spoke of this and she was intrigued, asking if she and Caroline (from Switzerland) could come with me. Caroline also had the same response and said in her limited English, "I don't know what you are talking about or what you are doing Cathy. I just know that I need to come with you. When the hairs stand up on my arms, I know that this is my truth."

So we all set off walking down into the village, and as we were wandering down the hill, I told them more of my experiences. Both women were captivated and resonated with my story. Here we were—three women from three different countries united in our quest for healing.

We found the stone in the middle of Forres, connected with each other by holding hands, and created an impromptu ceremony. We asked for the three of us to be disconnected from any negativity that had happened to us in the past, forgiving all who were involved, and to be reconnected to the wisdom of our souls. It was a powerful and unexpected experience. We must have looked very strange to the people walking and driving past—three women, standing around the stone, holding hands, with their eyes closed and in a world of their own.

We took photos and talked about the connection we felt with each other and the experience. I felt a deep sense of completion and knew that my week in Findhorn had concluded a mission I didn't even realise that I had been on.

As we walked back through the village, I told Dominique and Caroline about wanting to take a clay angel made in Findhorn home with me for my kitchen. My concern was that a clay angel made in Findhorn would be too heavy, since I still had four more weeks of travelling via Ireland and London. They laughed an assured me that I would find a way.

Leaving them at the weekend markets, I wandered back to Cluny Hill College, gathered my belongings, and waited outside for Raymond and Thelma. I sat on a bench in the garden, just outside the entrance to the building and observed the new people entering for their Experience Week. My thoughts reflected on how I had been just like them, entering into unknown territory and unaware of the limitless possibilities that waited. *Was that only one week ago?* So much had happened to me in that short time.

I watched one woman arrive, and after dropping her luggage off, she walked over and sat beside me. We smiled at each other and started talking. Jayne asked me to share with her my understanding of Experience Week. *What do I say? What do I share with this woman?* I hadn't yet integrated these experiences myself, so I explained to her that she had to have an open heart and mind, and she would get exactly what she needed.

We chatted for some time, and she expressed her appreciation for my advice. She said I had given her so much and that she felt she needed to give me something. Jayne then asked me to shut my eyes and put my hand out open in front of me. I was a little apprehensive when she asked me to do this but nonetheless followed her instructions. When she indicated that I could open my eyes, there in my hand was an angel, hand painted on a tiny blue ceramic tile. I stared at it in amazement, not believing what I was seeing. I nearly fell off the seat and couldn't believe what had just happened. Talk about manifestation!

If I could attract an angel as easily as that, what else could I do! How on earth could this woman have known I wanted an angel? I now had my Findhorn angel to take home. This tiny angel met all the criteria. She was delicate, yet strong enough not to break and hardly weighed anything, which would make it easy for me to carry her back home, halfway around the world.

Now this little angel still sits on the shelf in my kitchen, watching everything that I do and symbolises my unforgettable week in Findhorn. What a miracle.

I emailed Jim when I returned home to tell him of my extra adventures. His response made me laugh:

> How come you only found out about the Witches Stone once I'd left? I'm devastated that I wasn't one of those tuning in around the stone in full view of the wary Forres folk! That image of you guys there is powerful indeed. Two centuries ago, they'd have rolled you all down the hill, together in one tight barrel ...
>
> Now, your other stories about coincidences and connections are so familiar. I think we've all found such things happening to us, post-Findhorn, too many to be coincidence. I don't know what it is— Findhorn magic? Try explaining that to someone who's not been lucky enough to experience what we did. Impossible! We were so blessed by angels to have that life-changing experience.

I couldn't agree more. We were certainly blessed to have such exceptional experiences.

The Witches Stone in Forres, Scotland

CHAPTER 10

Cancer Support WA

History repeated itself. Ten years after leaving Cancer Support WA, I was invited back to work there once again. It seems a little quirky to me that I was offered the same job twice in my life. *Is this my "calling"?* It's not your run-of-the-mill employment. It is quite unique and specific in its needs. When I returned, the desk I used was exactly the same and in the same position as it had been ten years previously, looking out of the window to the neighbouring childcare centre. On my return, I experienced a strange sensation of being in a time warp. It was as though I had walked out the door one day, experienced ten years of life, and walked back in the next day. The only difference was the staff members, except for Mandy, who I had known briefly before I'd left the first time.

When I returned to Cancer Support WA, typical for a not-for-profit organisation, it was short of money again and was on the verge of closing down. This unique organisation that had helped save my life twenty years earlier was now in the throes of dying, and I felt it was my duty to help bring it back to life. I needed to do all that I could to help it heal and recover, just as it had been there for me, but I was also very aware that doing so would be an uphill battle. I sensed a feeling of loss and confusion within the organisation.

Cancer Support WA was founded in 1984 when Jill Mattioli

was running the Seekers Centre in Subiaco. At that time, the Seekers Centre was attracting people who were going through the experience of cancer and felt that there was something missing from their treatments. These people were seeking support mentally, emotionally, and spiritually during their time of treatment and knew that this kind of support was an essential part missing from their regime. Jill had heard about Dr. Ian Gawler and invited him to Western Australia to share his story. When the seminar finished, a small group of people were inspired and founded the Cancer Support Association of Western Australia.

Mandy, a friend and colleague of mine with similar beliefs and values, had spoken about taking the organisation back to its original source and intent, a sanctuary—a non-judgemental place where people could choose the way they wanted to deal with their cancer and feel supported regardless of their choices. The week after we spoke, mysteriously, the very first newsletter ever produced arrived on her desk, and to this day, we have no idea who put it there. When we read it, to our amazement, we found an editorial by Jill explaining the beginnings of the organisation. Mandy thought that it would be a good idea to reproduce this letter in the latest edition of the Cancer Support WA Wellness Magazine, and she was in the middle of typing the article when the receptionist rang through to say that there was a woman on the phone who had a query and could she please take the call.

Can you imagine Mandy's surprise when she answered to find that it was Jill! None of us had ever met Jill so we were amazed at this coincidence. We were excited by the reconnection and wanted to meet her. We invited her to the centre to share our vision with her. It was a special meeting and solidified the foundations for the rebuilding of the organisation.

I would like to share with you the article from the first Wellness News magazine in April 1984, written by Jill:

The Seed
by Jill Mattioli

I guess that the beginning of this Association, from my personal aspect began three years ago, in my early days of working at the Seekers Centre.

In February of 1981 a very dear friend and neighbour of ours attended a public hospital, was diagnosed as having cancer of the throat and received the treatments prescribed by the doctors of the establishment. On most visits, he was attended by a different duty doctor, none of which did much for his stability of mind or hope for recovery. It was relayed to me that on one of these visits he was blatantly told by that days' duty doctor that "he was going to die" and this he did in five short months.

During this time he did come to the Seekers Centre and received spiritual healing. This gave him the ability to pray again, something he had not done for many years.

Since Tom's passing, I have sat at my desk in the Centre's study many times and pondered deeply over an answer to the treatment, and success of such treatment of similarly afflicted sufferers.

Last July, I first read of Dr. Ian Gawler; and then again in September. On this second occasion I re-read in depth exactly what Ian was proposing that people can achieve a better quality and greater quantity of life, by simply taking more responsibility for the process of recovery, through meditation, diet, positive thinking and in many cases, a change of philosophy of life.

Perhaps there was the answer to the question which still lay with me?

I wrote to him, asking him to come to Western Australia. When after some weeks I had no reply I contacted a friend in Brisbane, obtained Ian's telephone number and called him direct, with the thought that perhaps something had happened to my letter—it had. Ian had misplaced it somewhere and had been endeavouring to make contact.

Then followed many telephone calls to organise the visit but no plans could be finalised since Gayle and Ian were expecting an addition to their family. At length a tentative date was set for the last weekend in January 1984 as Ian was to address the Vet school at Murdoch University, a date which was then changed to later in the year.

You see, in order to prepare the newsletter for January, I had asked for a firm decision from Ian. The opening of the Centre and the newsletter still had to go on and the newsletter was ready to be reduced, pasted up and delivered to the printers. Somehow I didn't get there. I fiddled around, chastising myself for being lazy.

One full week after the due date I got around to it. I got up to take things to the printers but the phone rang. "I'll be there on the original date after all," said Ian's voice. Now I knew why that newsletter had not reached the printers when it should have.

When his visit came nearer, Kim was one of the first to enrol in the weekend seminar. She spoke to me of how she and a friend Linda, also a cancer patient, had supported each other and found that their loads were lighter, their road smoother and that they had toyed with an idea to form a support group. We were able to make available our building etc. and could assist.

Looking back over the events that led to the formation of this Association, I see once again—as I have seen many times before—that when something is right, the pieces of the ensuing jigsaw all fall into place if we let it.

What is right will happen, if it is for the good of all and all will benefit by it.

*   *   *

As I had been associated with the organisation for so long, the president of the board had originally asked me to help guide Cancer Support WA back on track, but when I reported to him what I had observed and felt, he was not impressed and didn't want to acknowledge any problems. I made several suggestions to improve the situation, but they were ignored. So two other staff members and I requested a meeting with the board to air our concerns.

Unfortunately only two board members came to the meeting, and although we were bitterly disappointed with this outcome, we openly and honestly communicated our concerns. I was almost in tears, and you could hear the emotion in my voice as I desperately pleaded with them to do something to help us get back on track. Cancer Support WA meant the world to me. It had been the only place to give me hope when I was at my most vulnerable, and I wanted that sanctuary to be available for others in the future. It was my Findhorn in Western Australia, and I was going to do all that I possibly could to support it and allow it to return to its full potential. Cancer Support WA is a wonderful organisation, but unfortunately, not enough people know about it. Those who are fortunate enough to discover it are amazed at what they find.

Mandy and I were so unhappy about the events that had taken place that we decided to write another letter to the board detailing our concerns. This made our intentions clear and transparent and informed the board members, as we were not certain that everyone was aware of what was happening.

To say I was frustrated with all that was happening around me would be an understatement. I was racking my brain to find a way to change what was going to be an inevitable outcome—the closing of the Centre. I spoke to Mandy, and we decided that we had nothing to lose and the only way for the organisation to move forward was to get the members involved. We needed people who were committed to creating a place of healing—a place where people could come and *just be* and sort through the shock and confusion of being diagnosed with cancer, a place where they could empower themselves with knowledge and work through the many choices they now had to make about their lives, without fear of judgement about their choices and how they wanted to deal with their life-threatening situations.

We knew it was going to be difficult, but we were totally committed to finding another way the organisation could survive and flourish. There ensued many consultations and meetings in coffee shops with people in the community, who guided us and supported our cause.

We set off on a healing journey for Cancer Support WA. We found people who were willing to take on the challenge of helping a cancer organisation that was struggling to survive, and I can tell you, there are not too many people who have the courage and fortitude to take on a role like this.

My brother-in-law, Richard, volunteered to help. He had recently retired and had been a bank manager, teacher, lecturer, and professor at a university. He had also completed a doctorate in philosophy. No one else could have done what he did for the organisation, and I will be eternally grateful for his support. Richard and my sister Margaret have always been there for me, like a safety net, and I really appreciated all they did. I must admit I was shocked when Richard offered to take on this position, as it was well beyond the duties of a brother-in-law!

Pat, a friend and neighbour of thirty years, also offered to help. Pat is an engineer and embraced this very difficult challenge wholeheartedly, with the support of his wife, Jill. We managed to gather together six other amazing and dedicated people to assist us with this mammoth task.

Cancer Support WA now had life support, but it still had a long journey to recovery. There were many sleepless nights for all concerned and a lot of personal stress, but the underlying reason we had committed so much to this cause is that we believed in what we did and wanted to "hold the space" for this inspirational organisation.

It was at this time that my friend Ross Taylor (who is also a long-term survivor of secondary melanoma) was in negotiations with the National Trust to create the Cancer Wellness Centre at Wanslea, the hundred-year-old building. For the first time, Cancer Support WA, Breast Cancer Care WA, and Melanoma WA would all come together under the one umbrella and create the first "Cancer Campus" in Australia, where people diagnosed with cancer could access all services in one place.

The Lotteries Commission of Western Australia funded this project to the tune of eight million dollars, and the buildings were completely renovated and were officially opened by the premier of Western Australia in November 2014. It was a day I felt really proud. We had been running programs for the previous two years between the Cottesloe Civic Centre and the old buildings as they were being renovated. Sometimes the building site was absolute chaos as the transformation of these buildings and the organisation took place, and we were very grateful to the members who supported us and continued to come to our events and programs during this time.

We faced many other challenges during these four years, and I would just like to add here that I had a very steep learning curve, and I am very grateful to my incredible work colleagues and friends who witnessed the journey of Cancer Support WA through these times.

I love that, as an organisation, Cancer Support WA is

independent, even though that does cause some cash flow problems; it is free to explore life in a non-judgemental way and not only help thousands of people overcome some of the physical aspects of cancer but also assist them in finding peace in their hearts, minds, and souls—in a nutshell, their lives. I heard someone say once, "Some people heal and live, and some people heal and die." Death is not a failure; it is a part of life. To me, true healing is when people are at peace with themselves and the world.

Meeting with thousands of people over the last twenty-six years and facilitating groups at Cancer Support WA has enriched my life and given me much joy. As I write this book, my mind constantly drifts back over the years, remembering all the amazing and inspirational people I have met. It warms my heart to take time to reflect and remember their kind words, which make me feel humble. I feel this work is my life purpose and my calling. It gives meaning to all that I have experienced in life and makes everything I've been through worthwhile. It has become a sanctuary for many people from many walks of life.

I share below some feedback from members:

- "Thank you for your love, support and wisdom and also for teaching me that there is more than one pathway up the mountain."
- "Thank you for your wisdom, your inspiration, your beautiful heart and your sense of giving that touches me and so many."
- "Thank you for all your efforts and helping me get back on track."
- "Thank you, Cathy, for shining a light on my journey up the mountain."
- "Thank you for opening up a whole new world of learning and alternative way of doing things."
- "I found Cathy's content and delivery to be really great. One felt that she had without intruding into your space, a strong

benevolent invisible hand on your back, gently guiding you to a better place. She was assertive, empathetic, sensitive and kind."

- And from a grieving husband, "Thanks for that ray of sunshine and hope you gave to Marie during her time of illness. Without that hope your association instils, then people in Marie's situation flounder."

I treasure these words and appreciate that people have felt the need to express their gratitude, but I would like to say a big thank you to everyone who has trusted me to show them another way. This healing journey with Cancer Support WA has enriched my life to a depth I once again can't express in words, but I would like to say I have learnt so much from each and every person who knew there was more than just treatment to their "cancer experience." And I hope to continue to share the wisdom I have gained from these interactions with others.

The icing on the cake was when Cancer Support WA was awarded an Australia Day Award in 2014. Mike, a colleague and also long-term survivor of cancer, and I were asked to jointly accept this award on behalf of the organisation. It was a perfect January morning in the gardens of the Cottesloe Civic Centre when we were awarded the Town of Cottesloe, Australia Day Awards 2104, Community Group of the Year Award, "for continuous and tireless work over the last thirty years to support people who have been diagnosed with cancer, as well as their family and friends, within the Cottesloe community and surrounding areas; for their inspiring promotion of 'cancer wellness' to the wider community."

These words finally validated everything that Cancer Support WA represented and acknowledged the need for these services in our community. I was delightfully surprised to find out that we had also been awarded the Premier's Australia Day Active Citizenship Award for a Community Group. The wording on this certificate stated,

"Cancer Support WA, fostering Australian pride and spirit through active citizenship and outstanding contribution to community."

When I first walked up the stairs of this impressive building twenty-six years ago looking for hope, I was frightened, stressed, and living in despair with the prognosis I had been given. I wanted to know how I could extend my life a little bit longer so that I could see my beautiful children, Carolyn and Hayden, grow up and have the opportunity to know them as adults. They needed their mum, and I needed them. Today, my heart bursts with gratitude and love, as I have now witnessed them grow and develop into two exceptional human beings. I have watched them graduate from school and university and claim their independence by getting their driver's licenses and commencing their careers. I have witnessed their weddings and warmly welcomed their partners, Kevin and Cindy, into our family. And most of all, I am so grateful to be a grandmother to four beautiful souls—Olarni, Sterling, Chloe, and Eden. I love them all so much and will never be able to pay back to Cancer Support WA all that it has given me by teaching me another way to live.

I don't think that there is much more for me to say about the passion I feel for Cancer Support WA, except that for me it is a guiding light and a place of hope. Hopefully, my small contribution to its survival repays this priceless gift and means that it will continue for many years to come as a guiding light for others who have fallen into darkness and despair.

Me with my beautiful grandchildren,
Olarni, Sterling, Chloe, and Eden

CHAPTER 11

Transgenerational Healing

One of the most fascinating forms of healing that I discovered was transgenerational healing. This healing modality looks back over the lives of past generations and discovers patterns or events that have occurred and are yet to be resolved. A large part of our patterning in life stems from our genetic inheritance. In Western culture, we have forgotten much about this inner knowing. Three of my grandparents died before I was born, so I didn't know much about them. Several times over the years I had heard reference to transgenerational healing but took little notice of it. Coming across a book about healing the family tree stimulated my interest, and I was extremely lucky to still have many relatives in their eighties and nineties alive when I decided to take on the task of exploring and getting to know my forebears. My elderly relatives were custodians of old photos and stories, which I gathered from each of them and lovingly placed these precious fragments together. It was like a giant jigsaw, and when different parts came together, I started to get glimpses of the bigger picture of our family tree and lineage.

The table in my family room was covered in photos and documents for over twelve months, and I found the process of discovering more and more about the lives of my forbearers fascinating. It felt like I was going back in time, finding these ancestors, and introducing myself to them. Sadly, some lives were cut short, and I found within me a need to find resolution. If I had known how much hard work this process was going to be, perhaps I would never have started. But when it was completed, I was very proud of my achievement.

This process was documented for my children with a photo album and a file with all the relevant documents categorised. The theory is that, within a family, there is a direct link or chain of energy to each other. This energy is held within our genes. If this energy is left "damaged or incomplete," it can have an effect on future generations, so I wasn't only doing this work for myself; I was doing it for my children and grandchildren.

People are now more aware of the need to "find their roots" and are becoming involved with genealogy. Genealogy even gives us a clue with the word *gene* in its name. The meaning of the word genealogy is in the root *gene*, as in "passed on through the genes." Add to that the suffix *-ology*, which means "study," and you get genealogy, the study of one's origins. There is now awareness of *epigenetics*, where scientists are studying the biological mechanisms that will switch genes on and off.

One of the more interesting stories I found in my family tree when I was searching for healing came from the time when my father had left England, at only nine years old, with his parents and older brother. The family had left a beautiful farm in Leicester in the United Kingdom to become part of the Group Settlement Scheme in Pemberton. They arrived in Albany and were sent by train to Mandogalup (near Perth) and then back down to Pemberton, dropped in the middle of the forest, and told that this was their new farm and that, to make it work, they would have to clear the land themselves. The trees were massive Karri trees, and the family lived in a tent while they cleared the land for a farm.

After five years, eventually the farm became productive, and the family was just starting to feel settled when my grandfather, Tom Rate, went to a neighbouring farm to help a horse that was having difficulties. Being a very isolated community, everyone helped each other whenever they could. It was a Sunday morning, and Tom went across the road to his neighbours'. Unfortunately, when he walked behind the horse, it was startled and kicked its hind leg out, hitting Tom under the chin and breaking his neck. He died instantly, and the family was distraught.

My grandmother Mary was taken to hospital, as she was so overwhelmed by grief. The boys were left behind to run the farm, but it was impossible, as they were much too young and didn't have the experience needed to continue in this harsh environment. Unfortunately, the farm was sold, and the family moved on.

My grandfather was buried in the Pemberton cemetery, but there was not enough money for a tombstone, so he was buried in an unmarked grave. This tragic family story made me feel very sad, and I felt that I needed to honour my grandfather in some way for the sacrifices he'd made for us. I just didn't know how.

When I decided to go back and find my family history, my deceased sister, Kathleen, came up again. I spoke to Margaret and Richard, and we decided that we would try to find where Kathleen Jean was buried. Margaret rang the Pemberton Tourist Bureau, and after much searching, the person at the bureau was unable to find a grave for Kathleen Jean Rate, born and died May 7, 1944.

This was puzzling to us, so Margaret asked if there was a grave for Thomas Henry Rate (our grandfather). The bureau found his unmarked grave, only with a number and no other identification and informed us that they had discovered that "Baby Rate" was also buried in the same grave. This stirred a deep sadness within me. Two lost souls abandoned, members of our family, without even a plaque on their combined grave to mark that they had ever existed. Thank goodness they were together. My mum was eighty at this time, and we felt we had to give her some acknowledgement and closure for the traumatic birth and death of Kathleen. This was something that should have been done some sixty years earlier.

We told Mum what we had discovered and of the plans we had to place a small plaque on the grave to acknowledge the lives of these lost members of our family. Mum informed us that before my grandmother Mary died, she had asked my dad if he would mark his father's grave, as it was one thing she had regretted never doing. Unfortunately, my Dad hadn't gotten around to fulfilling his mother's final wish. It may have been too painful for him, as he was only young when his father died, and upon reflection now, I am sure that he would have still had unresolved grief from this tragic event.

Margaret, Richard, and I made arrangements to take Mum to Pemberton to say goodbye to her baby, and we wanted to acknowledge Thomas, who had made a very difficult decision to start a new life in Australia with his family and had paid the price with his life for helping a neighbour in need.

We set off on another healing journey—this time with a small plaque mounted on a concrete base among our luggage in the boot of the car. It was a crisp autumn day when, after much searching of the Pemberton cemetery, we eventually found the unmarked grave, neglected, isolated, and barren. Richard mixed up some instant concrete with a little water and secured the plaque on top of the small mound of dirt that outlined the grave. We also placed a small plant on top as a symbol of love and remembrance. Each one of us stood in silence, reflecting in our mind and hearts what this pilgrimage meant to each of us.

I silently thanked my grandfather for his decision to come to Australia, acknowledging his hardships and loss of life, and thanked him for giving me the opportunity to live in such a wonderful country. It made me realise that the decisions we make can have far-reaching effects into the future, affecting the lives of many people.

I also told Kathleen how much her life had affected me; that, even though she had been unable to take even one breath, her life had influenced many people; and that she was loved by siblings who did not even have a chance to know her. This was an emotionally stirring process, which I felt deeply in my heart. But strangely, there was also a sense of joy that finally we had connected, as much as this life would allow.

I don't know what the others said silently in their minds and hearts as we reflected on our losses in this quiet country cemetery. The only sounds I was aware of at the time were the wind as it rustled the leaves of the trees and an occasional bird singing its song in the distance. I don't recall who broke the silence and suggested that we move along, but I do know that I felt a sense of completion for me.

When we arrived at the motel, Margaret and Richard were in one room, and Mum and I were in another. I was looking for my walking shoes when Mum said to me, "I have to tell you something." I stopped what I was doing and listened as she continued. "I nearly didn't come with you this weekend, but knowing you and Margaret have gone to so much trouble, I didn't want to disappoint you both. I woke up this morning and I was bleeding. I was frightened and didn't want to be so far away from Perth in case I needed to go to hospital. I just want to let you know in case something happens during the night."

At first, I didn't quite know what to make of this but reassured her that she would be okay. This was an eighty-year-old woman who hadn't had a period for over thirty years, and the weekend we took her to the grave of her daughter who'd died so traumatically sixty years previously, she bled. *Is her body remembering this dreadful experience and releasing the energy and trauma locked inside her for so many decades?*

The afternoon was one of reflection as we sat watching the sun go down. It was a stunning sunset, with clouds stretching across the sky, illuminated by the sun, creating a palate of blood red and rich orange. It was a fitting symbol of closure for Mum and the grief she had been carrying with her for so long.

The next day, we searched for the ruins of the Rate family farm, and we were lucky enough to meet a man whose father had bought the farm after my grandfather died. I am grateful we met him. He knew the Rate family well and after much detective work on the old farm, found the stump of a pine tree that was planted out the front of the original house Thomas had built for his family eighty years previously. This symbolised the Rate family and the roots they had put down when they'd first arrived in Australia. Solidly, it stood there like a monument, marking for us the exact location of the house. Margaret and I stood proudly on either side as Richard took a photo. Unfinished business in our family tree felt healed and put to rest.

We drove back to Perth, and the following day, I rang Mum to see how she was. To her amazement and mine, the bleeding had completely subsided as quickly as it had started.

I found the courage to speak to Margaret about the experience that I'd had many years earlier, where I'd felt I was the baby left to die on the cold, stainless steel bench. She listened intently and without interruption to my story and simply replied, "I'm not surprised. Even though you are seven years younger than me, with what you say and how you deal with things, I sometimes feel you are older, like a big sister."

Her response was just what I needed. It was confirmation of what I had felt for a long time, without any ridicule or judgement. What a sister!

Who really knows how life works and why we exist? Life has many aspects, many of which are never explored or explained, and I feel very privileged to have had the opportunity in my life to explore these deeper levels. This healing modality is not for everyone, but obviously, it is something that I needed, and who knows what else will be revealed to me in the future!

Life is a miracle and something that should be relished. It was an honour and privilege to be present at the birth of my daughter's children. I was humbled to be there to experience the joy of witnessing these dear little souls take their first breaths of life. It is something very special to be reminded that the lineage of our family continues and that we are part of the continuum of life, ever changing and evolving.

CHAPTER 12

Journeys of the Spirit

As you may have guessed, the week in Findhorn was profound for me and opened up a doorway into parts of my being I never knew existed. I felt as though I had *found a part of myself* that had long been ignored. Intuitively, I knew there was a lot more within me I had to find and explore. My very deep yearning to travel to spiritual places around the world would not go away. Something was calling me to explore not only my inner world but also the wider world. I knew I didn't want to just be a tourist anymore, visiting and ticking off a list of places I had visited. I wanted and I needed experiences—experiences that would test me and bring to the surface aspects of myself that needed healing. It felt like some force was leading me on a pilgrimage, a transformational journey, where life-giving challenges would emerge. I needed to discover different aspects of myself and heal the parts that were lost or fearful or had been fragmented in some way.

Jim contacted me from South Africa to say that he was visiting his son in Perth, and was there an opportunity to catch up once again? Unfortunately his partner, Marlize, was unable to come, and as I had heard so much about her, I was disappointed she was not coming with him.

By coincidence, a New Earth festival was being held in Denmark, a small country town in rural Western Australia known for its "alternative" population. Jim and I drove down via Albany so that he could do a bit of sightseeing while he was in Australia. Arriving at the festival, we found about two hundred people from all walks of life—different and interesting people from all over Australia—and we found the music and celebrations stirring.

The most profound event for us was when a local Aboriginal elder welcomed us to country and performed a dance and very special ceremony. *Welcome to Country* is a ceremony performed by indigenous Australian elders to welcome visitors to their traditional land. It can take many forms, including singing, dancing, smoke ceremonies or a speech, depending on the particular culture of the traditional owners.

We were really touched by this ancient ceremony and felt privileged to witness and be part of it. This elder was accompanied by two women who had mixed ancient red earth into a paste and invited anyone who wished to be "reconnected to the earth" to join them. Jim and I looked at each other, nodded our heads in affirmation, and stepped forward; our faces were painted with this red earth as part of the ancient ceremony. I was moved as I reflected on the power of mother earth to provide us with everything that we need—food, shelter, and a beautiful place to live.

A duo called Sacred Earth was singing at the festival, and their music still stirs me today when I hear the chanting of their voices. This experience was very special and touched me deeply on an emotional level.

Jim invited me to South Africa in 2012. I had always wanted to go to Africa, so I jumped at the opportunity to explore this ancient land. It lured me with a sense of adventure and danger.

One of the highlights of my visit was when we visited a place called Maropeng, which means "returning to the place of origin" in the local African language of Setswana. This place was also known as the Cradle of Humankind, and UNESCO named it a World Heritage Site in 1999. Deep within the Sterkfontein Cave, there is a skeleton, which has been named Mrs. Ples. She is one of the oldest skeletons found and is estimated to be 2.3 million years old. Wow. I felt very humble being able to visit a place whose history extends to the beginning of humankind, the birthplace of humanity. While we stood in this sacred place, I realised just how insignificant I was in the vastness of the human race but that I was also an important cog of the continuity of the human race. We all are. I just hadn't realised it. Going to Findhorn had been like reconnecting back to my spirit, and coming here was like going back in time and acknowledging the source of my physical body. I felt a very deep connection between these two experiences and was grateful to have had them.

Another highlight was flying down to Cape Town for a week. When we arrived, Jim hired a car and drove directly to the basement of his apartment building in the centre of the city. The surprise I received as he opened the door to his apartment nearly knocked me over. There, directly in front, was the most magnificent view of Table Mountain I ever could have imagined. It was so close, in fact, that I felt I could reach out and touch it. Feeling overwhelmed, I just stopped and stared at this prominent landmark.

There is definitely something very special about Table Mountain. It is powerful and impressive, and we spent many hours sitting on the balcony meditating and watching the colour changes on the side of the mountain as the sun travelled overhead, casting shadows against the ancient rock. Sometimes, with my very vivid imagination, I could see the outline and profiles of ancient spirits dancing across the preface. I had to pinch myself to make sure I was really there. Three years earlier when my life fell apart, I couldn't have imagined myself sitting on a balcony in Cape Town, meditating, drinking good red wine, and having very interesting and stimulating conversations with a like-minded Scotsman who lived in Africa. You just have to love life and the surprises it presents!

The adventures continued when I was fortunate to travel to Tasmania with my friends Sue and Nick. This was certainly a journey to feed the soul. For me, Tasmania had everything a holiday destination could need. It has interesting history, beautiful scenery, amazing food, and exceptional wilderness.

One of the many highlights during our time there was hiring a yacht and travelling up the Gordon River overnight to one of the last remaining tracks of temperate rainforest left on the planet, also classified as a World Heritage Area. In 1982, there were protests to protect this part of the river from a hydroelectric dam being built. The movement that eventually led to the project's cancellation became one of the most significant environmental campaigns in Australian history. This pristine area was certainly worth fighting for, to preserve it for future generations. It is a powerfully evocative wilderness and one that resonated with a silence deep within me. The reflections of the trees in the water were spectacular and evoked a reminder for me to take time to reflect on my life and how far I had come since my life had changed so dramatically.

The rest of the two-week adventure was filled with exploring this beautiful island, as well as lots of fun and laugher. On the last day, while we were waiting to go to the airport, Sue, Nick, and I decided to go to a winery to fill in some time. Printed on the paper tablecloth were the words, "Good wine, good food, and good friends." I thought, *What more could I want?* My life had transformed so much that I could hardly recognise myself.

I went back to Africa again in 2013. This time I went to visit friends Colleen and Greg in Ghana for three weeks and then Jim and Marlize in Johannesburg for two weeks on my way home. I booked my tickets and asked the travel agent if I needed any visas.

She looked up some information on her computer and said, "No, all you need is a yellow fever injection, and here is the address for a travel doctor."

So trusting her, I organised everything and arrived at the airport full of anticipation of a wonderful adventure. When I enquired with the woman at the check-in desk whether I had to pick my luggage up for the ten-hour stopover in Johannesburg, she informed me that the airline could not take me to Ghana, as I didn't have a visa. I was flabbergasted and shocked so asked if I could get a visa for Ghana in Johannesburg. Her suggestion was that I go to the Ghanaian embassy when I arrive, as that was my best chance at such short notice.

The flight across the Indian Ocean was long, and as I couldn't sleep, I decided to read a book. Very tired and concerned, I arrived in Joburg at 5:00 a.m. after an eleven-hour flight and, after collecting my luggage, asked several people where the Ghanaian embassy was. All I got were blank looks and shrugging shoulders. I eventually found someone who told me that the Embassy was in Pretoria. I purchased a train ticket and, after transferring to another train, arrived in Pretoria at about 6:45 a.m.

The sun hadn't risen above the buildings, and it was a cold, chilly morning. As it was early, not many shops were open. Scouting around, I found a warm coffee shop, which felt like a haven to me. The smell of coffee was welcoming, and while I waited for the enticing brew to be delivered, I turned my iPad on to find an address for the embassy. Even though I found the address, I had no idea which direction it was in, so once again, I asked for directions.

Eventually, I found someone, who advised me I had to get back on the train and go to Hatfield, the last stop on this line. When I arrived, it was about 7:30 a.m., by this time still not many people around. People I chose to ask directions from couldn't understand what I was asking for, so I showed them my piece of paper with the address written down.

Unfortunately, none of them could read. They looked at me blankly, turned their back to me, and walked away. Eventually, I found a friendly man working on the side of the road who gave me directions to walk a couple of streets farther on and reassured me I would find the embassy on the right-hand side.

It didn't take long to discover, but it was still only 8:00 a.m., and the embassy didn't open until 9:00 a.m. Tired and hungry, I sat perched against the wall with my backpack and purple suitcase by my side. The guards with their guns were watching me with great interest, but no one approached to ask what I was doing. I did have a few of the local people walking by stare at me, wondering what on earth I could be up to. It must have been a sight to see me there.

When the embassy eventually opened, I rushed in and asked for a visa, as my connecting flight to Ghana was leaving at 6:00 p.m. that day.

The woman just stared at me without any sympathy and said, "We only issue visas here to South Africans, and it takes three days." She also informed me that I would have to return to Australia to get one.

My stomach dropped at this news, and no amount of sweet-talking could convince this woman to give me a visa today.

Feeling very dejected, I turned toward the exit. As I walked out, I stopped and asked one of the other officials where the Australian embassy was, as I felt I had nowhere else to go. With great authority, he informed me it wasn't far away, so I asked him to draw me a mud map. This map directed me past the University of Pretoria and then indicated that, several streets farther on, I would find the Australian embassy on a corner, on the right-hand side, just past a main road I would have to take care crossing.

Off I set once again, with my backpack on and dragging my purple suitcase behind me, through the streets of Pretoria for an hour and a half until I finally reached the embassy. I was so relieved to find it, as many of the locals were stopping and staring at me, the only white woman walking in this area by herself with everything she had in her backpack and suitcase.

I entered the building thirsty, heart beating fast, red-faced, hot, and sweaty. Several booths were open, so I chose the shortest queue. When I finally got to the embassy official, I hastily told her my tale of woe, hardly taking time to draw breath.

She looked at me bewildered and said, "I'm sorry, dear. This is the Austrian Embassy, not the Australian Embassy."

What?! You have got to be kidding!

She felt very sorry for me and tried to be as helpful as possible by printing off a map of Pretoria and marking the Australian Embassy on it for me. I couldn't believe it. There it was marked in red pen, back on the opposite side of town, around the corner from the Ghanaian embassy? *Bugger!*

I was exhausted and went outside to ring Colleen and Greg to inform them that I wouldn't be on the flight to Ghana that afternoon and that I was going back to find the Australian embassy. I promised them that I would keep them informed of my whereabouts. Greg said that Colleen wasn't well and they may have to fly back to Australia before I could get there, but he would try and get me an emergency visa through the company he was working for in Ghana. I must admit that, by this time, I was feeling isolated and didn't know what to do, as Jim and Marlize were in Cyprus and weren't expecting me at their place for another three weeks.

I rang Jim's office to find out exactly when he and Marlize were returning but was informed that they wouldn't be back for some time. As I hung up the phone feeling hot, tired, and confused, a lovely Austrian couple in their seventies approached me and said sympathetically, "You look like you are in a bit of trouble. Can we help you?"

I must admit I was a little sceptical. Here I was in a foreign land, no one knew where I was, and here was a couple offering to take me to the Australian embassy in their car. It was April 25, Anzac Day, which is an important national holiday in Australia, marking the first major military action fought by Australian and New Zealand forces during the first world war. I wasn't even sure whether the embassy would be open, but I felt travelling with the couple was safer than trying a taxi.

The last thing my anxious and fearful ninety-year-old mother had said to me as I left was, "You're not going to be alone, are you?" I had reassured her I would be with people all the time, and here I was, all alone and stranded. Mum would have been full of fear had she known what was happening. Reflecting back on this experience, perhaps I was feeling alone and stranded in my life, and this adventure was just bringing these feelings up for me to examine and heal. Intuitively, I knew I had to face my fears to move forward in my life.

I thanked the Austrian couple profusely when they dropped me off at the Australian embassy. This very sweet couple were like angels sent to guide me to my destination. Sometimes in life you need a little help to get where you want to go.

After many phone calls, the Australian government official confirmed that the only way I could get a visa to Ghana was to go back to Australia. *No way.* I was not travelling this far and going back without having a holiday, so I thanked them for their assistance and found my way back to the train and returned to the airport. Where else could I go?

I didn't want to waste my money so decided I would change my flight and go to Victoria Falls in Zimbabwe, a place I had heard about and wanted to explore. It was on my "bucket list," so this seemed like a good alternative. Arriving back at the airport, I changed my ticket and caught a taxi to a nearby shopping centre and made arrangements for accommodation in Zimbabwe. By the time this was arranged, it was dark outside, and once again, I found myself alone, this time standing outside the shopping centre waiting for the taxi, which was stuck in traffic.

As the flight for Zimbabwe didn't leave until the next day, I booked myself into a hotel at the airport. At 8:00 p.m., I finally lowered my weary body into a bath filled up with warm, soothing water and contemplated my situation and processed the events of the day. I was physically, emotionally, and mentally exhausted. On the flight over to South Africa, I had read a book by Wayne Dyer called *There's a Spiritual Solution for Every Problem.* What a coincidence to have read a book like this on my way over. Basically, Dyer was saying that the more you remained calm and "centred" in life, the more connected you were to your inner guidance and intuition; and the more stressed and agitated you were, the further away you were from this inner guidance and the more likely you were to make compromising choices. *Easy*, I thought, *I'll just meditate, stay calm, and allow this adventure in Africa to gracefully unfold.*

I woke up the next morning, meandered through the airport, and found my way to the plane for Zimbabwe. After a bit of a mix-up regarding me changing the ticket the night before, I was finally on the plane, upgraded to business class, and smiling to myself that this must be the shortest flight I had been on and the only one ever upgraded. I will have to work at getting an upgrade on a longer flight next time.

I arrived in Zimbabwe and was taken to the Kingdom Hotel, just a short walk from the mighty Victoria Falls. I could hear the roar of the water as it cascaded over the edge of the fissure in the earth, sending up a cloud of mist that looked like smoke in the distance. It is known as "the Smoke that Thunders."

I sat on my balcony and absorbed the atmosphere, reflected on my journey so far, and wondered why and how on earth I had ended up here. I sent an email to my family titled "Greetings from Zimbabwe," which set of a ripple of concern through the family, with my daughter phoning my sister to enquire whether she knew any more about why I was in Zimbabwe and not Ghana! Even though I was fifty-seven years old, I requested that they don't tell Mum what had happened. She would have been beside herself with worry.

I made my way down to the falls through a bush pathway at the back of the hotel and was absolutely mesmerised when my eyes fell upon the sight. It was beyond spectacular, and there aren't words to describe it. You have to experience it to understand the sheer power and incredible volume of water and its overwhelming size. Life had gone to extraordinary lengths to get me here, and I wasn't going to waste a moment of it. I noticed there was an excursion where you could fly over Victoria Falls in a helicopter. It is known as "the Flight of Angels," and it certainly had a heavenly feel about it. I needed to do this just to get some sense of proportion and the grandeur of this magnificent place. My soul was soaring as I flew over this sacred place.

Each night at the hotel there was a cultural performance, and when I heard the drums and the singing start, I would make my way from my room to the balcony above the stage, where I sat back and enjoyed the sound of deep voices chanting and the slap of the dancers' feet upon the ground as they danced, sang and celebrated life.

I had seen promotions for a trip to Chobe National Park in Botswana while walking around the dusty streets of Victoria but had dismissed it as impossible for me, as I'd thought getting a visa would be difficult.

The second night I watched the cultural performance, a local tourist guide walked past me, stopped, and turned around and said, "You wouldn't want to go to Botswana, would you?"

I couldn't believe it. My immediate answer was, "Yes!"

He picked me up from the hotel two days later; drove me to the Zimbabwe/Botswana border, where I paid for a visa; and, after crossing the border, found an open safari vehicle waiting for me. We drove to a resort on the side of the Chobe River, and it was one of the most memorable places I have visited. The area was teeming with animals in the wild as they came down to the river to drink and wallow in the mud. The morning was spent in a small aluminium boat, floating along the river, birdwatching, and observing hippopotamuses and crocodiles as they sunned themself in the mud on the banks of the river. I loved watching the elephants at the water's edge. It was like witnessing a reunion of lost friends as they reached out with their trunks and greeted each other. The afternoon was spent in the open safari vehicle as it drove through the park, tracking animals, and giving us all an opportunity to witness these beautiful creatures in the wild, the way nature intended. This was a day I would remember with great affection. It was like visiting the Garden of Eden.

As I packed my bags, ready to return to Johannesburg, Jim

rang to say that he and Marlize were back, and he would collect me from the airport. I was relieved because Greg had phoned to say that Colleen was extremely sick and they'd both had to fly back to Australia immediately. I had felt that something was stopping me going to Ghana, and now I understood why. It was just as well that I had decided to "go with the flow" and see where this journey took me. I had experiences that were beyond my wildest dreams.

Jim and Marlize's home was bliss. They were very welcoming, but I did feel like I was imposing on them for these extra couple of weeks so asked where else I could travel while I was there. They suggested Mauritius, so back to the airport I happily went.

My next stop was a week of luxury living in a resort that looked like it was floating on water. It had more swimming pools than I had ever seen in one place. It is amazing where you can end up when you just let go and trust. *Ah ha*. Another life lesson learnt. Mauritius was beautiful, and I enjoyed exploring and drinking in the atmosphere.

One of the highlights was snorkelling. I felt I was in another world under the water, silent and beautiful, a magical place to "just be."

On my return to South Africa, Jim and Marlize took me to the Welgevondon Game Reserve, where we stayed at Nedile Lodge, winner of the Best Game Lodge in South African at the 2014 World Luxury Hotel Awards in Cape Town.

This place was luxury plus, in a unique setting that could not be replicated anywhere else. I love the saying on the lodge's website (an African proverb according to the site): "You must treat the Earth well. It was not given to you by your parents—it is loaned to you by your children."

I soaked up the experience and went on every three-hour safari, morning and night, for the five days we were there. Driving through the bush searching for the big five—elephants, lions, leopards, buffalo, and rhinos—was so exciting. I can only claim to have seen four and a half, as when we found the leopard, it was in long grass, and all I got to see was its tail poking out of the grass as it was meandering along! I also loved the giraffe and our wonderful guide, Michael, would suddenly stop and jump out to bring the local flora to us for examination. He was an encyclopaedia of knowledge.

One morning, Jim decided to come with me. It was a very cold and uneventful morning until we were on our way back to the lodge. We saw a huge bull elephant on the side of the track. What we didn't know was that he was in musth (a periodic condition in bull elephants characterised by highly aggressive behaviour and accompanied by up to a 60 per cent rise in testosterone).

Michael stopped the brand new Range Rover we were travelling in so that we could take photos. He turned the engine off, and as we were sitting there quietly admiring this wonderful beast and absorbing the smells and sounds of the African bush, suddenly the elephant turned around and charged at us. He was very angry and ready to kill. A powerful aura of energy surrounded him, and as he started to run, you could feel this energy, like a cloud of dense matter filled with testosterone and anger.

Michael was desperately trying to find reverse in his new chariot, and when he did, he planted his foot, and we were travelling in reverse at about forty kilometres an hour, with this very large and angry elephant chasing us, trumpeting and projecting fluid from his elevated trunk toward us and looking enormous with his outstretched ears.

I think that I got closer to death that day than I had when I was diagnosed with cancer. My heart started to race, and my stomach churned as I dropped the camera on my lap and held on tight. There were no seat belts in the vehicle. My knuckles were white as I gripped the railing in front of me. I remember thinking in that moment, *I didn't think my life would end like this.*

The elephant was gaining on us and getting closer and closer, but thankfully we eventually outran him. He stopped and casually turned around and started walking away from us along the dusty track—swaggering with an air of triumph that he had gallantly chased away this annoying intruder that had invaded his territory.

We were in shock. One young couple on their honeymoon sat there holding each other. Another lady was shaking and said her whole life had just flashed before her eyes. I looked around to find Jim with his camera in his hand. He had taken three fantastic photos as the elephant charged us and got closer and closer. All that Jim could think of at the time was, *This is interesting!* He also told me later that his life had flashed before his eyes, but he only had time to get up to the age of six.

It took over an hour to travel the last few hundred metres back to the lodge. We kept well away from the elephant as he sauntered along the track. There was a welcoming party when we returned. The staff was waiting anxiously for us, as Michael had called ahead on his radio to alert them of our predicament. They were very relieved that we had returned safely, and so was I.

Jim's photo of the bull elephant starting to charge

Gaining momentum

One very angry elephant in full flight

The following weekend, Jim and I set off to Ixopo in the KwaZulu-Natal area to the Buddhist Retreat Centre. Marlize left her cosy bed at 4:30 a.m. to see us off, and as we drove down through the Drakensberg Mountains (a name derived from the Afrikaans word meaning dragon), I don't think I have seen a more beautiful sunrise. The mountains were huge and dark, and when the sun rose behind them, my imagination ran wild; I was sure we were surrounded by mystical dragons. It was sensational, and I could see why these mountains had been given their name. What an unexpected experience on our way to Ixopo, but it was only a taste of what was to come.

We arrived at the retreat and could understand why Nelson Mandela had declared that it was a Natural Heritage Site. The Buddhist Retreat Centre is positioned on the side of a mountain, at the head of a valley in the Umkomaas river system. CNN featured it as one of the ten finest meditation centres in the world, and I know why. The sights of the garden are amazing, the smells of the flowers waft in the air, and the playfulness of the monkeys as they chase each other around can do nothing but bring a smile to your face.

Jim and I were there for three days, and on the first day, I remember sitting on a bench overlooking the valley meditating, when the sounds of the Zulu's chanting and singing in their village came dancing up in the air from down in the valley. This was surreal. Here I was in Africa, meditating at a Buddhist retreat, overlooking a spectacular valley, listening to sounds that touched my soul. I was mesmerised and present in the moment. Nothing else existed except for me and this moment.

We were fortunate enough to be there at Wesak, which is the day that Buddha's birthday is acknowledged. In the evening, the group did a meditation, and as we filed out of the meditation room, we were handed some incense and were silently directed to walk a path that had been illuminated with candles. At the end of this path was a four-metre high Buddha, which we walked around three times before placing the incense in a container. There was a full moon (which marks when Wesak will be held) and not a breath of wind on this perfect night. It was a sacred and special ceremony, and when it finished, the group gathered together and lit candles under paper-thin lanterns, which then gently floated up toward the stars and full moon. It could be nothing else except a magical moment in my life.

The journey of my soul was creating some balance to the grief and pain I had experienced. I felt so alive and happy. My past was healed, and it was time to move forward. I simply wanted my soul journey to unfold. No expectations. No limits. Just trust in a process that I was beginning to understand. Life is good and certainly a gift to be treasured.

CHAPTER 13

The Retreats Continue

After returning from South Africa, I found myself in Bali two months later. Mandy, the CEO at Cancer Support WA, had asked if I would like to host a retreat in Ubud, within the mountains of Bali. It is a spiritual place and a wonderful place to relax and heal. I was happy to pay for my own airfare, so I booked my flights and waited in anticipation for people to book in to join me on the retreat.

Unfortunately, at the time, we didn't have the resources to promote the retreat sufficiently. We had some interest, but only one person booked, so the retreat was cancelled. This didn't deter me at all. I was looking forward to two weeks by myself, so created my own amazing retreat, which I enjoyed immensely. I hadn't been to many retreats in my life, and here I was, travelling from one retreat to another. Life was presenting me time and space to reassess my priorities and teach me many lessons from internal and external exploration.

My life was now on track and 2013 turned out to be a great year. It started out really well when I received an email from Ian Gawler in January, asking whether I was interested in joining him in Central Australia, and assisting at a meditation retreat he and his wife, Ruth, were hosting in September. His offer was too good to refuse (not that I even considered not going for a second), and when he asked at the end of the email if I "was in," my reply was a resounding "yes."

I could not believe it. Here was Ian Gawler asking me to assist him as one of four leaders at a meditation retreat for thirty-six people. My mind reflected back twenty years to the time when I was first diagnosed with cancer. I had been stressed, distraught, and fearful, when someone had told me about Ian and given me one of his tapes. I remember lying down on the floor in my lounge room and placing the cassette in the player. A very slow, methodical voice came out of the speakers, and I checked to see that I had inserted the tape correctly. All was okay, so I continued on, and Ian's voice led me to my first experience of meditation. He took me to such a deep level that I was not even aware of my body. At this time, my future was uncertain, and I had no idea of what lay ahead. I could have never imagined at this time that I would someday work with Ian, running his program in Perth and then assisting him with meditation in one of the most isolated and ruggedly beautiful places in Australia.

The day before the retreat, Ruth and the other local counsellor, Michael, drove me out to Hamilton Downs Youth Camp, which was an hour and a half drive from Alice Springs. The cook, Ken, and his German backpacker assistant, Sven, were already there, scrubbing up the kitchen and getting everything ready to prepare delicious vegetarian food. The three of us spent the first night preparing the campsite for the arrival of the participants the following day. I was excited when the bus arrived in a cloud of red dust, and I was honoured to welcome them to this very special place.

Bunkhouses were available for people to sleep, but most people, including myself, chose to sleep in a swag on the nearby ancient riverbed, sleeping under the stars, not just five-star accommodation but million-star accommodation. Lying there at night, I could hear dingoes howling in the distance, and with all of this surrounding me, I felt I was "at one" with the environment. It made me realise how vast the universe is and left me wondering about the presence of the source that so finely organises everything. How could I not be in awe? I am such a small part of something great. The words of Desiderata kept repeating in my mind: *You are a child of the Universe, no less than the trees and the stars; you have a right to be here. No doubt the Universe is unfolding as it should.* So much wisdom in words, and here I was experiencing it, going beyond the words.

Ian and Ruth were aware of each participant's needs and gave 100 per cent of their attention to each person. I was thankful to be part of this group and fascinated by the sight of forty people sitting in the middle of the desert meditating together. I know that there are many references in history to people "going into the desert or wilderness to find themselves." What insightful people Ian and Ruth are to create this opportunity for people to have this experience. The effort to organise such an event is phenomenal.

One of my favourite activities involved each of the leaders taking nine people to sit in a circle on the dry riverbed. One session was held during the afternoon and another one in the evening around a campfire. Each person was given one hour to tell his or her life story. It was an honour and privilege to be in this space. People were open, honest, and transparent as they relayed their journey. There were many tears and much healing. Each story had an impact on me at one level or another. I cannot write this book without acknowledging the sacredness of this experience. In the darkness around the campfire, we could not see the faces of people as they relayed their stories, but we could sense their souls—that sacred part that is buried deep beneath the pain and suffering of existence.

Meditation takes you to that place, when you give yourself the time. It takes you down through the deeper levels of the mind to that silent, sacred part that is deep within all of us—that elusive part that is just waiting for you to take the inner journey of discovery and reconnection. For me, cancer was the catalyst that initiated my quest. The healing didn't come from the outside; it came from within. The doctors couldn't do it for me, the naturopath couldn't do it for me, and Ian couldn't do it for me. Each of these people was holding a mirror for me to see what I hadn't discovered within myself. They were the signposts on *my* journey of healing and self-discovery. Everyone's journey is unique; we are all seeking the same destination—unconditional love, peace, harmony, and meaning to life.

Ruth was formerly a GP in Alice Springs and had built up a wonderful relationship with some of the indigenous elders in the area. She arranged for these elders to join the retreat for the last three days. I felt privileged when we were invited to sit with them in their camp. Very few people are granted this exceptional experience. Each day, we sat with them and watched as they did traditional painting, explaining the symbology of the patterns emerging on the canvas.

One piece spoke to me, and I knew I had to take it home. It was painted by Johnny Possum Japaljarri from the Yuendumu Community and was called "Janganpa Jukurrpa" (Possum Dreaming). I asked the significance of the patterns and was told they were the signs on a map of the possum's journey. For me it represented my soul journey, and here I was at the centre of the country with indigenous elders sharing their wisdom, life, and ceremonies.

This painting now takes pride of place on the wall in my office, reminding me of this special experience.

The men separated from the group and went down the creek bed to do "men's business," while the women stayed in the main camp doing "women's business." We hunted for witchetty grubs, which are the most important insect food of the desert and have historically been a staple in the diets of Indigenous Australians. The red earth was as hard as concrete, so the aboriginal women produced a couple of crowbars to dig at the roots of the witchetty bush. As they searched the roots of the bush, large bulges in the roots were found and forced open to reveal big, fat, white witchetty grubs. These were taken back to camp and roasted in the coals of the fire. To me, they were tasty and surprisingly similar to peanut butter.

The following day was a day of ceremony. The men went off to their camp once again and ceremoniously painted so that they could dance for the women. The women would also dance for the men and were to be painted accordingly. There was no pressure, and the invitation was given to those women who wished to experience this ceremony to present themselves naked from the waist up. Some women refused, and I must admit that I was a little hesitant at first, until I saw 90 per cent of the women taking their tops off. I admired their courage, as some had had full mastectomies, some had had part of their breast removed, some were very buxom, and others had very small breasts. I decided that I wanted to be part of this ceremony, as perhaps this would be the only time in my life I would have this experience.

The elders mixed up the paints and began singing and chanting as they painted each woman's breasts and face. As each person moved herself forward for painting, these incredible elders did not hesitate when they were confronted with chests that were scarred and had missing breasts. These scars represented the wounds each had experienced during her battle for survival. These caring women were not interested in the physical aspect of the woman in front of them; they were respectfully acknowledging her spirit. I witnessed how much Indigenous Australians are connected to the earth and nature. They are part of the earth, and the earth is part of them.

With the painting completed, we sat back and waited for the men to dance for us. It was a very special moment as we watched them walk down the ancient riverbed toward us. Each man had been ceremoniously painted, and they chanted with their deep voices as they danced the ancient ritual.

Then it was our turn to dance for the men and I think it was one of the most liberating moments of my life. Our faces were red— not from embarrassment but from the hot Australian sun. For me it was about letting my spirit be free—free from all the beliefs and conditioning that had been pushed upon me. Free from the "body beautiful" expectation. It was lovely to finally be free to be "just me."

We packed up camp and made our way back into Alice Springs by bus. As I boarded the plane for the return flight to Perth and to my life, I realised that I had evolved into a different person. I may have looked the same on the outside, but something had changed within me.

Mandy and her husband own a yoga centre and periodically took groups of people to India for retreats. I was talking with her one day about this and said I would like to join her next time she went, as I hadn't yet visited India.

She said, "No."

I was at first taken back that she didn't want me to go with her, but this wasn't the case. Mandy wanted me to take people on my own Ayurvedic retreat. I was very excited. She asked me to contact Julie Baker at Journeys of the Spirit in Perth, who organised unique travel experiences for groups.

In September 2014, I led my inaugural group to Kerala, India. This was where Ayurveda originated five thousand years ago. I was in my element. Ten people and me! Eleven in numerology is a gateway, and this was my gateway to another level of awareness. Julie arranged a health resort for us, which had won awards for ten years as the "Best Ayurvedic Resort in Kerala."

Each person had his or her own hut overlooking the Arabian Sea, and the sound of the waves crashing upon the beach went continuously, like a constant healing chant in the background. Over many years, Julie has built up an incredible relationship with these people, so on the first day, the doctors do a blessing for all groups that came under the banner of Journeys of the Spirit. We lined up opposite the Ayurvedic doctors, and one of the doctors, who was in his eighties and had been practising Ayurveda for over sixty years, led a beautiful and moving ceremony, welcoming and blessing us.

In Ayurveda, (ayu means life and veda means the knowledge of) health is defined as the dynamic state of balance between mind, body, and environment. And from the five elements, the three doshas—vata, pitta, and kapha—known as mind-body types, are derived.

On arrival, participants were asked to fill out a form and have a consultation with one of the doctors. Each person's body type was ascertained, and a treatment plan was created specifically for him or her. People were encouraged to share their experiences with each other but asked not to compare, as everyone is an individual and has different needs, even those who have the same body type.

Meditation started the day at 7:00 a.m., along with pranayama, which is the formal practice of controlling the breath and is the source of our prana, or vital life force. Nothing is compulsory, so it was entirely up to the individual whether he or she wished to participate.

The group met for breakfast at 8:00 a.m. and enjoyed freshly prepared foods. Each dish was labelled with a body type (vata, pitta, or kapha) so each person selected food that was best for his or her body. There were also many delicious dishes that were common for all.

Chakra meditation at 10:00 a.m. was popular, and this was a process where people were guided by a teacher to open up energy centres within the body. Chakra translates as "energy wheels," and chakras are believed to be part of the subtle body, not the physical body; as such, they are the meeting points of the subtle (non-physical) energy channels called *nadi*. Nadi are believed to be channels in the subtle body through which the life force or vital energy moves.

Every day at 10:45 a.m. saw people dressed in maroon gowns and waiting to see their doctor, as each person's health was monitored and changes were made to the treatment plan if required.

Everyone welcomed 11:00 am, as we were guided to the treatment rooms by our assigned practitioner. My treatments lasted each day from one and a half to two and a half hours, depending on the treatment. These sessions started with herbs being placed on my crown chakra (the top of my head) and the therapist chanting a blessing. Oils mixed with suitable herbs for my dosha were massaged into my body while I sat on a chair. I climbed onto a table, where two women massaged me, one either side, mirroring the other. This was absolute bliss!

My treatments varied and included milk baths, reflexology,

facials, body scrubs (with herbs and lemon wrapped up in cheesecloth), body rubs (herbs and warm oil in cheesecloth), and saunas. My favourite treatment was a copper pot filled with warm oil, suspended over my face before the warm oil flowed over my forehead and flushed away the stress. This Shirodhara technique soothed and invigorated my senses and mind and took me to a level of relaxation beyond imagination!

After the treatments, and still cocooned in maroon gowns, with cheesecloth wrapped around our heads, holding herbs on our crown chakras, we made our way to lunch. The afternoon was "quiet time" so the oils could work their magic. This took the form of swinging in a hammock, lying on a bed, writing a journal, or meditating.

I generally took a shower at 3:00 pm, ready for late afternoon yoga. Following yoga, the pool lured me to cool off on the way back to my cottage.

It was then time to meet with the group. The retreat is built on a high feminine energy lay line, so we would sit on the ground and connect directly to the earth. This was the time for people to share how they were experiencing this beautiful place and catch up with everyone else.

Dinner was a time of gathering to share delicious food from the buffet. Sometimes, there were thunderous tropical storms at this time. But if it was fine, the tables were set up under the stars, and the evening concluded with cultural entertainment.

Some of the group found it relaxing to do a bit of retail therapy out in the streets, bartering with the locals. However, shopping is not for me. The streets were filled with the sights, sounds, and experiences that only India can deliver.

Kerala was the perfect place for me to offer each person an individual "energy session," where I shared my skills of hypnotherapy and reiki. Seven of the ten accepted this offer, and I must admit that I felt as though I had reached a pinnacle in my life. Here I was, in an exotic country, with an inspirational group of people, doing what I loved best. I could never have imagined anything more perfect. How much better did life get than this?

*   *   *

Well, it did get better. After lots more travelling to Canada, Alaska, and Chile, I ended up at Machu Picchu in Peru. I spent five days with a Peruvian shaman, who guided me to many Inca sites throughout the Sacred Valley. My time with him was very special, as he explained to me many of the hidden symbols within these picturesque areas of the Andes Mountains.

When we finally reached the top of Machu Picchu, I could not help reflecting back on my cancer journey. Over the years, I have always told people that there is not just one way to overcome cancer, as it is a complex illness, and that there are "many pathways up the mountain." It took me twenty-six years to get to the top of my mountain, and I could never have guessed or known the many pathways I would have to take to get there. Each pathway (experience) taught or revealed to me something about myself, and the internal exploration has been as vast and varied as the experiences I have had externally while exploring this wonderful world.

I know that, in my future, I will continue travelling and taking people on retreats. This will also include visiting incredible sacred places, where retreat participants, too, can experience this beautiful and diverse world and be inspired to explore, express, and expand their inner world at the same time. My message to you is to let go of fear and *trust your intuition and the process of life.* You never know where it will lead you.

Machu Picchu, symbolic of having reached
the top of my mountain

CHAPTER 14

Remembering

I first met Christine Morrison when Jim and I attended the New Earth Festival in Denmark. Christine has the ability to see into your light and soul and express this vibration as music. She has the voice of an angel, which helps to heal people and sooth troubled souls. I clicked with her instantly, but with both of us having busy lives, unfortunately, we didn't make the time to catch up with each other for quite some time. We bumped into each other again a couple of years later, and Christine enquired how I was going. At the end of this conversation, I purchased some of her CDs and was deeply touched when she gave me one of her "Soul Impression" sessions as a gift.

As I walked into her room, there was a faint smell of essential oils and a feeling I had entered somewhere special. At the start of my session, Christine spoke with me about my intent and what I would like to achieve from this experience. We developed the affirmation, "I am connected. I am at peace, all with ease and grace."

With this agreed, I found myself sitting in front of her, the two of us connected to each other not only in spirit but by the headphones that connected me to her electronic piano.

As I sat back, relaxed, in a very comfortable chair, my ears were filled with the most beautiful music I have ever heard, coming through the headphones as Christine played to me the music she felt intuitively. Tears trickled down my cheeks. These weren't tears of sadness; they were tears of joy, and of remembering. This was the music of my soul. The music churned emotions deep within, and I recognised these vibrations as unconditional love. I allowed myself to be embraced by the love and strength emanating through her. There was no sense of time, and I was surprised to discover that I had been in this space for thirty minutes.

With the session concluded, I sat there speechless. *What can I say following discovery of another dimension of myself?*

Early in my search for health, I had heard that healing comes from within, and what I discovered is that, the more you look, the more you find. The mind is far more intriguing and complex than we can comprehend.

Luckily, Christine copied the session onto a CD for me. At home, when I need time to relax and centre myself, I play this music and find myself floating through the day without a care in the world.

With all of the healing modalities that I had investigated over the years, I had never come across anything as unique as this, so you can imagine my surprise when, a month later, Ian Gawler posted this article on his blog, *Out on a Limb*:

Finding our True Identity

Consider this. When is a baby first conceived?

Imagine this. A woman decides she will have a child. Conception? She takes herself off and sits under a tree, listening for the song of the child that she will conceive. Once she hears it, she goes to the potential father and teaches him the song. Then they make love, pausing along the way to sing the song together. The couple sing the song to invite the child to join them.

The woman is in Africa, a member of the Himba tribe and this is how they do it.

Once the woman is pregnant, she teaches the child's song to the midwives, the older women and other members of the village.

The child is born to the welcoming sound of its own song being gently sung by all those around about. As it grows, if it should be injured, face a transition like puberty or marriage, or does something wonderful; the child receives the support, the acknowledgement, the honouring of the people it knows through the agency of them singing its song.

Similarly, if at any stage in its life this person should do something inappropriate—a crime or something socially unacceptable—the villagers gather, form a circle, install the person in the centre and sing them their song.

Correction through love. And affirmation of identity. And a reminder of connection and the truth of belonging. Gentle correction. Loving correction.

So the song is sung throughout life, and finally at the time of dying.

Different cultures have different traditions, but maybe something resonates when we read of such an extra-ordinary tradition as this. Maybe some yearning or nostalgia swells. A recognition of the value of connecting to the heart and how we need to be on guard to maintain this connection in a busy, largely secular world.

But then maybe too, it is as simple as taking ourselves off on our own from time to time and sitting silently. Maybe listening for our own song, or having it sung to us, is just one way of being reminded of our true identity and what is in our heart's essence?

Yes! This article explained what I had experienced but didn't know how to articulate. We all have a song to sing, and I believe that is why we are here on earth. The word *uni-verse* can be broken down to *uni* (one) *verse* (song). Life keeps trying to remind us of this contract, and Ian Gawler seems to always pop in and out of my life, showing me the way, blissfully unaware of his impact.

Modern medicine comes from a scientific and evidence-based model, which is suited well to treat injuries, illnesses, or diseases that match this paradigm. My belief is that "energy medicine" will be the medicine of the future. This isn't New Age; it is a sacred and ancient wisdom returning to remind us that individuals are unique and need to remember how powerful they are in creating this existence.

Life has many dimensions, and there are some aspects that will never be validated by science. But that doesn't mean that they don't exist; it just means that they can't be measured and categorised. Please don't get me wrong; it is not my intention to criticise medicine. I am just pointing out a difference and suggesting that outcomes may be better if the whole person was taken into account and both healing modalities were accepted and integrated.

Many people have told me that I was brave to turn my back on conventional medicine and rely solely on complimentary therapies. This is not my perception. I used the health system and allowed it to take me as far as it could, but when I felt abandoned, when there was nothing else science could offer me, I turned to complementary therapies. Through my strong willpower and knowing, I looked within myself and discovered my own pathway into this energetic realm.

Thoughts, beliefs, and emotions change the vibrations contained in this energetic realm. Resentment, hatred, overwork, fear, jealousy, and stress vibrate at a lower level than does optimum health. The antidotes to these behaviours are meditation, prayer, peace, kindness, and love. Subtly raising the vibrations that heal on many levels, creating "vibrant health," may be a new concept, but it is one worth contemplating. Overcoming a life-threatening illness is not solely about surviving; it's also about thriving.

I know many people who are fearful and stop living at a young age but keep breathing and existing until they're eighty—frightened to live their life to its full potential and express their true selves and living lives of fear and mistrust.

I have also met many exceptional people who love and embrace this world, trusting and making the most of it, and never complaining or playing the victim role.

Alf was an exceptional example of someone who didn't forget who he was and what life was all about. The first time we met, he told me he wanted to live to be a hundred. He was ninety-five when he came to Cancer Support WA, grieving the loss of his beloved wife. When he was speaking affectionately about her one day, I could sense his loss and see the pain on his face. Reminiscing briefly with me of their time together, he spoke of the wonderful paintings she had created and asked whether I would visit his house to view them. Feeling his pain, I agreed to visit and have a cup of tea with him after work.

As we sat together, Alf opened up about his life. I was stunned and saddened as his tragic story was relayed to me. When he had finished speaking and took some time for a deep breath, I questioned him, "Alf, how could someone go through so much and still want to live to be a hundred? I listen to people's tragic stories every day, and just one of yours would push many people over the edge."

He looked me straight in the eye and said, "Cath, I have the best friend in the world who helps me."

This response intrigued me as I thought he was isolated and lonely.

"It's Jesus," he explained. "Every night, I go to bed, I tell him my troubles, and I hand them over to him. I ask him to get back to me in the morning if he needs me to do anything. And do you know what? In ninety-five years, he has never got back to me. He has handled them all."

I smiled. Here was a man who had found a way to let go and move on with life, regardless of what had happened.

Alf loved life, grew his own vegetables, came to the centre for reiki, and eventually died, one week after his hundredth birthday. He maintained his vibrant health until the end.

What a great man and valuable lesson he taught me that day. Every morning is a new start; if you can find a way to leave the past behind you and stay true to yourself, then you're on the right track.

Witnessing and sharing in people's lives has been a privilege. Each person has taught me about the complexities and challenges of life and the struggles life can bring. What I find most rewarding is when people listen and remember their song. This remembering comes in many forms and can transform people's lives. Some people change their employment and take a chance with a new project, others leave relationships as their song is out of tune with people around them, and some simply blossom from the knowledge that they are enough and don't have to prove themselves to anyone else.

Just imagine a world where we are taught to trust life and not fear it; where we know how to release tragedy and grief from our energetic field; and where the important people around us learnt our song, just like in the Himba tribe in Africa, and sang our song with us when we were lost.

I know I was lost when I was diagnosed with secondary melanoma. I focussed solely on survival so that I would have the opportunity to see my children grow into adults. What I didn't know then was that I needed more than to just survive. I needed to thrive and grow and remember my song and say *yes* to opportunities that came my way.

CHAPTER 15

Full Circle

Cancer has taught me much about life and living consciously. I remember the first time I attended a support group and someone said, "The best thing that ever happened to me was that I got cancer."

I looked at her and thought, *You must be sick to believe that!* I wouldn't even wish cancer onto my worst enemy.

However, I am now grateful for my cancer experience and the way it has enriched my life. It has empowered and inspired me to focus on living in the moment and allowed me to create an amazing life for myself.

Friends say to me, "I want what you have, but I just don't want to have to go through what you went through to get it."

If you want to get "it," I suggest you learn to meditate. This may be challenging for some people, but meditation is a powerful tool. It is vital to give the body and mind a rest, especially since today's society places so much pressure on the need to *do* rather than to *be*. After all, we are *human beings*, not *human doings*. People don't expect their mobile phone to last without recharging it daily. That is how I view meditation. It is a time to recharge and allow my mind to find focus and balance again.

In every situation there is a positive and negative—night and day, sweet and sour, hot and cold. If your mind is focussed on the negatives, retrain it to focus on the positives. I remember travelling to Bali many years ago and taking photos of the stunning sunsets, the thick green forests, the exotic people, and everything I saw that gave me pleasure. I showed these to some friends who were excited by these photos, and it inspired them to book a trip to Bali.

When they returned, they were bitterly disappointed. I was shocked by their response, but when I viewed their photos, it all made sense. There was an album filled with pictures of broken drains, tangled electricity wires, dogs with scabies, and piles of rubbish. This aspect of Bali was their focus. What a shame they missed out on a wonderful holiday. It's not what you look at; it is what you see. Bali can be anything you want it to be. Look for it, and you will find it. Life is like that too. Look for the wonder in life, show gratitude for what you have, and you will be surprised how quickly life will change.

My life has been very rich with experiences and extremely rewarding since I altered my perception. I had no idea what was required for me to heal, and I didn't have any inkling of what would be involved in the process. I trusted a little voice inside me that didn't speak with words but with thoughts, feelings, and images. This is my intuition. Many times my experiences didn't make sense in the logical part of my brain, but they made sense in my heart. This was my journey, and I followed my heart. Everyone's healing journey is different, and judgements should never be made. I suggest to people I meet that they share their experiences with others but don't compare. We are all unique and individual.

Life has taught me many things. My first important realisation was that I needed to take responsibility for my own life. This is self-mastery. I believe that, when people change their perspective from a view in which things happen *to* them (which makes them victims and brings feelings of hopelessness and helplessness and an inability to change) to the view that everything that happened in their life happened *for* them, to help them grow and become empowered, life changes. This perspective can only come when there is a sense of being beyond the body and beyond the mind, an awareness of a power higher than yourself. There are many ways to discover this spirituality. Some find it through religion, some by meditation or through yoga, and others through reiki and other healing modalities. It doesn't matter how people connect. Yes, there are many pathways up the mountain. All that is needed is willingness to change and a commitment to make some effort.

Many people ask me, "What was the one thing that helped you overcome cancer?" There was no one thing, and there was no "magic pill." I felt like I was on a boat that had hit a reef; it had many holes ripped into the bow and was sinking fast. Cancer Support WA repaired one hole, meditation another, nutrition another, and reiki another (this was my healing team, which developed and evolved), until it could finally float again and continue on the journey through life.

Is nutrition important? Absolutely! Am I going to tell you what to eat? No way! There have been thousands of books written about nutrition by people who have spent their lives studying this topic. I know what worked for me and realise that I am not qualified to inform others. However, I have witnessed many people improve their health dramatically by eating organic, whole foods, free of poisons and pesticides. A helpful acronym tells us to eat SLOW food—food that is seasonal, local, organic and whole. The more that food is processed and interfered with, the harder it is for the body to assimilate. Look at the food you are about to eat and ask yourself, *Is this food life giving or life taking?* You will intuitively know the right answer for you. There are many products on the supermarket shelves that claim to be food. These packets of highly processed substances filled with preservatives, additives, and sugar are not food. They are "stomach filler" and have only been produced by companies who want to make money for their shareholders with these addictive substances. They are not the least bit interested in your health. Choose your food wisely, as you are the only person who can decide what goes in your mouth. Sourcing a good naturopath or health professional who can guide you through this minefield is a good investment of your time and money.

I remember a dear old couple, Tom and Mary, who attended my support group many years ago. Walking into the room, I was very concerned to see Mary crying. My first thought was that she had been given some distressing news regarding her cancer, so when the group commenced, I asked her whether she would like to share what was happening.

Both she and Tom had been very diligent with nutrition and took this aspect of healing seriously. Between sobs, Mary "confessed" to me that she had drunk a cup of coffee and eaten a biscuit during the week and was feeling very guilty. I felt sorry for her—that she had responded this way—and reassured her that the coffee and biscuit was not going to harm her but the emotional distress she was feeling would. She was relieved to hear this. If you choose to indulge occasionally, take the food in with love and joy, not fear and dread. Enjoying a cup of coffee with friends once a week can also help to feed your soul. It is much better to be out with friends and having a treat than to be isolated at home drinking a green tea and feeling utterly miserable.

Imagery is another integral aspect to healing. At one retreat I attended, when I was newly diagnosed, I was asked to draw my cancer. My first thought was one of resistance. *How on earth am I supposed to do that?* I thought.

After much contemplation, I proceeded to draw a simple mushroom with three strokes of my pen. I then added lots of little dots around the base of the stalk. For me, this simple mushroom represented the melanoma, and when it had been excised from my arm, it had dropped its spores, which had then travelled through my body and continued to grow. As all the conditions were perfect in my body for growing cancer, it had kept on spreading. My aim with nutrition and mediation was to change the chemistry of my body, so that the conditions changed and it wasn't conducive for the melanoma to grow. Keeping a mushroom farm dark and moist provides the perfect conditions for the mushrooms to grow. If they are taken outside in the sunshine and opened up, the soil dries out, and the mushrooms die because the environment has changed. This was my imagery for healing. Obviously, the conditions were perfect for melanoma to grow in my body, and I was desperate to change those conditions in any way possible. I vowed to do whatever it took, and I did it!

When the body is stressed, there is the process of fight or flight. This response originates back to the caveman days, when, if confronted by a sabre toothed tiger, the caveman had a choice—fight it or run away (flight). Whichever choice was made, the arms and legs needed all the blood flow and energy to function, so the digestive track closed down. This means that, if you are stressed, your digestive system is compromised, and you will not be absorbing all the nutrients needed to fuel a healthy body. Many people begin their healing journey with the major focus being on nutrition. This is a good start, but if you are not relaxed when you eat, your body is not absorbing the nutrients you have gone to so much effort to prepare.

Learn to relax. I know this is easier said than done, but all bodily functions work better when relaxed. Meditation was my choice to create peace within me. I had a selection of tapes and CDs, and I would ask myself, *What do I need today?* Sometimes I needed a man's voice to guide me, sometimes a woman's voice, sometimes music, and sometimes silence. I kept searching until I found which would be the best option for me on that day. Some took me to a deep state of relaxation, where healing could occur easily, simply, and effortlessly, and then there were others that irritated me, so I threw them away. The tapes were like trainer wheels on a bike. They kept me upright and balanced until I could manage to meditate by myself.

It is not my intention to simplify the seriousness of an illness, but the word disease can be broken down to *dis-ease*, meaning that something is not at ease. When you are at peace and ease with life, you don't have dis-ease. If you choose to deal with disease holistically, you need to address your body, mind, spirit, and emotions daily.

Here are some simple but very powerful *suggestions* which may help you to acknowledge and connect with these different aspects of your being:

> *Body* – nutrition, exercise, relaxation
> *Mind* – meditation, affirmations, visualisation
> *Spirit* – meditation, prayer, gratitude
> *Emotions* – gratitude, affirmations, expression

Think of the word emotion (e-motion) as short for "energy in motion." Finding a safe way to express emotion is essential. Many people have experienced tragic events and, at the time of the tragedies, didn't know how to effectively deal with them. So, as a way of coping, this emotion was tucked deep down into the body or mind and life carried on, expecting everything to be okay. Unfortunately, sometimes the unresolved and unexpressed emotions sit there and fester. Then, when least expected, this bottled-up anger rears its ugly head as disease and robs us of health and sometimes life.

One very expressive client, Geoff, gave a great analogy when diagnosed with cancer. He said "Cath, it was like the doctor took the safety pin out of a hand grenade and passed the grenade over the desk to me. I took hold of it very carefully, so it wouldn't explode and then took it home and handed it to my family and friends. I just didn't know when it would explode and destroy them as well." Emotions can be just like that. We don't know when they are going to explode and destroy. I believe that is why people are so scared of them and will do anything to avoid expressing them—anger in particular. People will go great lengths to avoid anger, either in themselves or others. There is nothing wrong with anger; it is what you do with the anger that can be destructive. Anger can be used in a positive way and, throughout history, has made many positive contributions to the world, especially when people unite and protest against an injustice. It is when anger is used to hurt yourself or other people that it is not okay.

A fun way to deal with anger that is being directed at you by another person is to use your imagination and imagine that you are bending over and saying to them, "You are obviously very angry and are trying to throw your anger at me. I don't want to catch it, so I am bending over for it to fly right over the top of me and disappear." Don't let other people dump their emotions on you and spoil your day. We are not in control of other people; we are only in control of our response to them. There is a difference between responding and reacting. Responding means that we hear what they are saying and respond back in a mature manner. Reacting means that we are re-enacting something that is not resolved within. Responding is empowering. Reacting is dis-empowering and leaves people feeling frustrated and unsettled.

I was very lucky to have a wise doctor in a cancer support group many years ago. During a discussion on emotions, he shared this enlightening story, which highlighted the fact that what you feel is not always about a situation or another person.

A group of people was sitting in a circle talking. Suddenly, Diane jumped up, grabbed Harry, and started dancing and being silly in the middle of the group. When they eventually sat down, each person was asked, "What did you feel when Diane and Harry were dancing?"

These were their answers:

DIANE. I felt *happy*, because it reminded me of when I was young and used to dance and have lots of fun.

HARRY. I felt *scared* and embarrassed, because I would never normally do anything like that.

ANNE. I felt very *sad*, because it reminded me of my daughter, who used to dance, and now she is sick and unable to walk.

NORM. I felt *bad*, because it reminded me of just how long it has been since I have allowed myself to have fun and just relax.

JIM. I felt *angry*, because I was enjoying the conversation, and when they got up and danced, everything changed.

FIONA. I felt *glad*, because it reminded me just how lucky I am to have such a healthy body and good life.

One of the men then turned to Diane and said, "Aren't you clever, being responsible for making *all* these people feel *all* these emotions?"

The moral of the story: Our feelings and emotions are more about us than other people and can be a good indicator of what is happening in our lives, pointing us in the right direction to understand and heal unresolved issues.

When I am with people and they start crying, I encourage them to feel what they are feeling and express it. I don't see crying as a breakdown, I see it as a breakthrough into the deep feelings and emotions which may have been buried for a very long time and need to be safely expressed for healing to occur.

Forgiveness is one of the most important and powerful tools when healing unresolved emotions. Unfortunately many people are confused by this word. When you forgive someone, you are reclaiming personal power that you feel has been stolen from you, *not* saying that what the person you're forgiving did or said to you was okay. Forgiveness is saying, "I am empowered now and release you from whatever you may have done to me, either knowingly or unknowingly. I am ready to move forward in my life and cut the emotional and mental ties that bind me to my past." The experiences of your past don't actually exist anywhere else except in your mind, so when you keep ruminating over painful past events, you are contaminating the present moment with this toxic energy. Releasing this tie may take a lot of work energetically, but doing so is essential if you want to live with peace in your heart, mind, and soul. If you find yourself righteous about what others have done to you, please remember that there may be people holding grudges against you within their body and mind that you don't know anything about. This mindset is not hurting you; it is only hurting them. There is a quote that sums this up well: "Resentment is like drinking poison and waiting for the other person to die." This is so true. The thoughts and feelings you have cascading through your body only affect your body and have the ability to either heal or destroy.

It is the same with words. Your words have an energy that can either heal or destroy. Be mindful when you speak, as this energy is like a boomerang and can come back to you in unexpected ways. Reclaim your personal power and don't hand it over to anyone else. Become the master of your own destiny and use it to create the life you desire. This may mean letting go of some people or situations in your life. I was once told by a very wise person, "There are only two ways to create and live your life. One is from fear, and one is from love and trust." When you are aware of this and empowered, you realise that it is your choice. We can't always control other people or what happens, but we can control how we deal with it. My interpretation of fate is that it is the direction in which your life moves without making any effort. That's your fate. Fate can be negative and is defined as the expected result of normal development. Destiny is your potential waiting to happen, but you have to be willing to take risks and put in effort.

Many years ago, there was a woman in my group who had finished all her cancer treatment but was fearful of the cancer returning and couldn't successfully re-engage into her life. Being fearful is a normal and natural response; only this woman was caught in her fears, and no amount of discussion or reassurance could settle her. Her husband was working as an engineer in Vietnam and wanted her to join him, but she would not go, just in case the cancer returned. We had Ajahm Brahm, an extremely wise Buddhist monk and Abbot of the Bodhinyana Monastery in Serpentine visit the centre, and at the end of his presentation, he asked if anyone had any questions.

This woman's hand shot up and she relayed her story to him. He asked her what her biggest concern was and she replied, "What if my cancer comes back if I join my husband in Vietnam?" He replied to her with a smile, "What if it doesn't?"

This was an "aha" moment for her and also something that I have incorporated into my life. My mind has the ability to create all sorts of imaginary fears, leaving me paralysed to live my life to the fullest. Now, when I hear the words in my head, *What if this happens?* I cancel it out with, *What if it doesn't?* I have found this to be a wonderful antidote to my internal fears.

It was never my intent to write this book to advise anyone on how to live his or her life. I don't have the solutions for others' problems, but if sharing my journey through life can show people another way, so be it. I would like to invite you to search deep within yourself, beyond the obvious, and discover who you truly are and find meaning and purpose in your life.

I do not know what my future holds, and living with uncertainty is okay for me now. I know that, one day, this life of mine will come to an end, and I hope I can lie on my deathbed and feel that it has been a life well lived and that I have made a difference. I hope that I don't look back with regrets and think, *I wish I had ...* Life is filled with experiences and adventures. But most of all, I appreciate the wonderful people who have been part of the weaving of my life. I will not take any material objects with me when I die. I will only take the memories of experiences and unconditional love.

It was while I was in India reflecting and contemplating my life that I decided to finally write this book. As I sat overlooking the Arabian Sea, intently listening to the incredible stories people were telling me about their lives, I was deeply moved by their insight and strength and willingness to share. This experience was surreal. I felt as though the same person was coming to me over and over, yet each story was unique. It was then that I realised that we all have stories, but we are not the story. We are souls experiencing life on earth. Each experience is unique. *Why is this so?* We bring with us the lessons we need to learn, and then life teaches us about forgiveness, compassion, unconditional love, or whatever it may be we need to learn. Life happens *for* us to grow and become whole, not *to* us to make us victims, feeling hopeless and helpless. The key to living a happy, healthy and abundant life is to change your mind by changing your perception. This creates inner peace and the ability to handle any situation.

My realisation was that I was full of stories and still hanging onto them. To move forward, I needed to process and release them. I am not the stories. I am more than stories. It was as though my spirit entered my body at birth, organised these experiences to teach me what I needed to know, and if I didn't learn from them and let them go, my life would become painful and stagnant. I was full and needed to create space for lots of new energy and experiences to come through me. That is why I decided to write this book. There was a strong need to let go of the many stories I held and create space within my being to discover and experience many more exciting aspects of life.

In January 2011, I purchased the run-down beach house from Mum. My son, Hayden; his wife, Cindy; and I spent many long hours over the next couple of years restoring and renovating the house by knocking down walls, painting, replacing the kitchen, and remodelling the bathrooms. This was all happening as I was restoring and remodelling my own life. My home is my peaceful sanctuary, completely restored now and a metaphor for my life. As I sit writing this book as a celebration of being free of secondary melanoma for over twenty-six years and celebrating that I am turning sixty, I reflect on the beginning of my healing journey and smile when I think about the butterfly landing on my shoulder at the hospital. I was scared, living in fear and uncertainty, having just been diagnosed with terminal cancer at the age of thirty-three, and I marvel that I now feel grateful for all the experiences this life has given me. There is a process in Japan called *Kintsukuroi*, where broken pottery is repaired with gold and so becomes more beautiful for having been broken.

My life was shattered several times, and I now feel that it has been repaired with gold. It is a beautiful life, enriched by gratitude for my children, grandchildren, family, and friends—a meaningful life with a deep sense of purpose. And I don't think there was any other way I could have understood and connected to myself so deeply. I now feel empowered and filled with love for life, trusting in a process of allowing my soul journey to unfold in the years ahead of me, just as it should. Not only did I survive secondary melanoma, I thrived. I can't believe that this journey began because of a little red dot on my arm.